The Military in African Politics

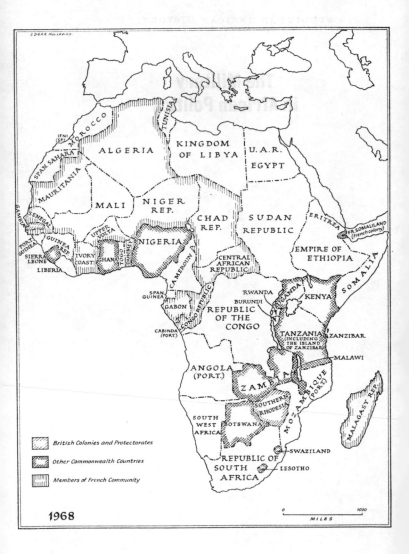

EDGAR HOLLOWAY.

IFNI (SP.)

MOROCCO

TUNISIA

ALGERIA

KINGDOM OF LIBYA

U.A.R.

EGYPT

SPAN SAHARA

MAURITANIA

MALI

NIGER REP.

CHAD REP.

SUDAN REPUBLIC

ERITREA

FR SOMALILAND (French colony)

GAMBIA

SENEGAL

PORT. GUINEA

GUINEA REP.

SIERRA LEONE

LIBERIA

IVORY COAST

UPPER VOLTA

GHANA

TOGO

DAHOMEY

NIGERIA

CAMEROUN

CENTRAL AFRICAN REPUBLIC

EMPIRE OF ETHIOPIA

SOMALIA

SPAN. GUINEA

GABON

CONGO REPUBLIC

REPUBLIC OF THE CONGO

RWANDA

BURUNDI

UGANDA

KENYA

CABINDA (PORT.)

TANZANIA (INCLUDING THE ISLAND OF ZANZIBAR)

ZANZIBAR

MALAWI

ANGOLA (PORT.)

ZAMBIA

MOZAMBIQUE (PORT.)

SOUTHERN RHODESIA

SOUTH WEST AFRICA

BOTSWANA

MALAGASY REP.

SWAZILAND

REPUBLIC OF SOUTH AFRICA

LESOTHO

British Colonies and Protectorates

Other Commonwealth Countries

Members of French Community

1968

0   1000

MILES

WILLIAM GUTTERIDGE

THE MILITARY IN AFRICAN POLITICS

METHUEN & CO LTD
11 New Fetter Lane · London EC4

First published 1969
© 1969 by William Gutteridge
Printed and bound in Great Britain
by Richard Clay (The Chaucer Press), Ltd., Bungay, Suffolk
SBN (casebound) 416 12430 5
SBN (paperback) 416 12440 2
Distributed in the USA by Barnes & Noble Inc.

Contents

Preface

This book is an attempt to assess the nature and importance of some of the recent incidents in Africa involving the military in politics. Because the subject is still, and is likely to remain, topical, a combination of a historical approach with political analysis has seemed the most profitable procedure: the fact that in most cases the situations described are still evolving has meant the leaving of loose ends. Reliable official sources of information are inevitably scarce and heavy reliance has had to be placed on Press and other reports and on conversations with observers. Research bulletins and digests, when compared and contrasted, have proved most useful, but the consistent thoroughness of the journal *West Africa* in publishing day-by-day reports from critical areas has been especially valuable.

Once again my wife and daughters have shown great tolerance of my absorption. I am most grateful to Miss Jill Francis for typing the whole piece.

April 1968   W. F. GUTTERIDGE

I · The Origins and Nature of African Armies

Since 1957 most sub-Saharan African countries have become independent of imperial rule and their governments have had to face the task of converting colonial institutions into national organs or replacing them altogether. For a number of reasons the adaptation of the armed forces to meet these new circumstances has been a slow process. As the penultimate instrument for the purpose of enforcing administration they were necessarily closely identified with the foreign rulers, who were naturally not anxious to have to bring in forces of their own soldiers from outside. Indeed, from the first the development of local military forces had been essential to European imperial domination in Africa.

In the decades before the First World War, when rapid expansion into the hinterland of Africa was taking place, units of troops and police had been raised *ad hoc* to meet particular needs and subsequently consolidated and regularized into official formations. Though there were differences in policy and practice as between the French, the British, and the Belgians in Africa the initial effect was much the same. Military service whether volunteer or conscript became a feature of African life which affected the political, economic, and social structure of society and provided an opportunity to individuals for a new kind of experience. For the imperial powers the establishment of political control would not have been practicable without locally recruited soldiers. This was certainly true of French West and Equatorial Africa as well as of British West, East, and Central Africa.

In the somewhat arbitrary administrative units of which the new states are today the successors, little distinction was at first drawn between civil and military administration. Military officers were prominent in the government of provinces and the administration of justice and occasionally civilians directed military expeditions. Parts of French Equatorial Africa were under military administration until after 1918 and for a long period in many areas the military and police rôles were mingled. Indeed policing in the form of the establishment of law and order and the putting down of the slave trade in, for example, Nyasaland was the *raison d'être* for such forces. Though they came ultimately in the world wars to serve imperial strategic purposes, they were not raised with this end in view but to free metropolitan troops for this more significant rôle. In the event of severe internal disorder, too, imperial reserves could be brought in, though this was rarely necessary. The results were, therefore, local military establishments generally barely adequate to meet the needs of internal security. Here some distinction must, however, be drawn between British and French policies as they developed during the first half of the twentieth century. For the British raised regional forces in Africa, notably the Royal West African Frontier Force (R.W.A.F.F.) and the King's African Rifles (K.A.R.), while the French recruited to the metropolitan army, albeit on terms which were different for European and African soldiers. The rate and extent of French recruitment was linked to global needs even outside the periods of the world wars. During times of peace far more African soldiers from French-administered areas were engaged in military service than from British colonies, but the latter tended to be more closely identified with their countries of origin. Even the British forces, however, were organized on a regional basis, though units and subunits were recruited territorially.

The formation of the West African Frontier Force (later the R.W.A.F.F.) was ordered in 1897 by Joseph Chamberlain, then Secretary of State for the Colonies. The force was consolidated by the end of the last Ashanti War in 1900 and by that time most units had already had some service in other territories. In Nigeria, the Gold Coast, and Sierra Leone constabulary forces had been raised at different times by local administrations or by the trading companies. The new force was based initially in Nigeria partly because of the existence of the longstanding Lagos, Royal Niger, and Oil Rivers Constabularies: there was also the threat of French rival claims for territory and the immediate availability of Captain F. D. Lugard as first Commander. The creation of this regional force was an important decision. Eventually Headquarters West Africa Command was established in Accra and remained there until Ghanaian independence was imminent in 1956. A combined training school was also established in the same vicinity. This regional organization may well have encouraged a degree of professionalism among West African soldiers; it certainly helped to promote close relationships between the military leaders of the various countries. Without it the interventions of General Ankrah in the deteriorating Nigerian situation in 1966-7 would scarcely have been possible. This is a practical example of the unpredictable ways in which decisions taken to suit imperial purposes have contributed to the post-independence situation. Other much more subtle influences emerge from a study of the evolution of military institutions in Africa over the relatively short period in question. It is important that these should be analysed pragmatically rather than in accordance with some preconceived pattern and to appreciate that for those expatriates who took the relevant decisions the prospect of independence for African territories was remote.

In the first years of its history the W.A.F.F. was used, as the constabularies had largely been employed before, for expeditions to establish British rule on the frontiers of empire. It served mainly in Northern Nigeria and inevitably left behind memories of punitive activities which were to affect, years later, the attitudes of local peoples to the army as a career. Of greater political significance was participation by British African troops in other territories and overseas. Though in one sense mercenaries, they gave generally extra-ordinarily loyal service in strange places – especially under General Smuts in German East Africa in the First World War and in Burma twenty-five years later. They served imperial needs and in many ways benefited from the experience. That they were volunteers was an important factor in this as a contribution to subsequent stability. Like the Indian Army, the African forces provided to a degree, regrettably minimally effective in Nigeria, a melting pot of the local races and ethnic groups. Individually ex-servicemen came to command a respect which has often given them significant status in sub-sequent developments. Not only have they had ready access to 'positions of trust', but they have had political influence in many areas. The overseas service of the R.W.A.F.F. and the K.A.R. in India and Burma from 1943–5 gave them 'a window on the world' at a point where political consciousness was seething on the surface. The exact nature of the contacts with the Indian Congress Party which took place then is not im-portant: the eyes of Africans were opened to political develop-ments in another part of the world while at the same time they were able to observe the sapping of the myth of European invincibility by an Asian power, Japan.

In many ways, in spite of the greater reliance on conscription, French military development in Africa was parallel to the British. Conscription itself, in fact, generated political con-sequences in that it and French reliance on African troops were continually used as bargaining counters to secure con-cessions with regard to citizenship and the franchise. The overall effect of intensive exploitation of African able-bodied manpower was not adverse to France's interests. There was political opposition to the use of French West African soldiers in North Africa and for the Suez operation, but in 1940 Equatorial Africa had provided spontaneous support for Free France and at least 10,000 men from there served in General Leclerc's army, many of them taking part in the celebrated march across the desert to Bir Hakeim. In spite of discrimination in conditions of service as between black and white troops, resistance to military service in some areas of the Ivory Coast, Dahomey, and elsewhere, and neglect until after 1948 of veterans' grievances, the French-speaking armies of Africa have retained an affinity to France and their leaders an identification with the French establishment unparalleled in Anglophone areas. The effect of this on their political behaviour may already have been significant. The direct influence of the soldier and the veteran on local politics followed from the preferential franchise which was allowed. In 1939 in West Africa all those who completed military service were rewarded with the right to vote. Ten years later in Dahomey 58 per cent. of the 54,000 electorate were ex-servicemen or serving soldiers. In Equatorial Africa, however, the franchise was not extended to soldiers as such until 1946. Other steps were eventually taken in both regions which tended to consolidate a military community. A mission under Commandant Henri Ligier was sent to Africa in 1948 to make a census of veterans with a view to resolving their grievances. Offices to deal with veterans' affairs were set up and club houses built. A proportion of jobs in the public service was reserved for ex-servicemen and low-cost housing was sometimes provided.

These welfare reforms and a considerable modification of the categorization of soldiers which had discriminated against many Africans followed upon the establishment of the Military Defence Committee of Central Africa in 1950. There was at this time a marked change in French attitudes to the military problems of the area as Africa assumed some importance for NATO strategy and Western security generally. The co-incidence of this change with an intensification of African political activity did not seriously limit its effects. It is true that the employment of African soldiers in North Africa and at Suez encountered strong opposition from a number of quarters and that in Equatorial Africa the 'Rassemblement du Peuple Français (R.P.F.)' tried to make use of veterans' organizations for its own political ends to the extent of occasionally holding meetings in the offices of the official veterans' welfare organization. Propaganda with Arab sympathies, however, had little success among non-Muslim soldiers in Sara Country from whence many recruits came. Wounded ex-servicemen were exempted from poll tax and in one region villages were actually built for their rehabilitation and residence in a semi-military environment. Thus circumstances in parts of French Africa combined to isolate the military from the rest of the community in a way which made their adaptation to the needs of post-independence society to some extent more difficult. Nor were army units transferred to the control of new states as of right on independence day as happened in British-controlled territories. It was often, as in the Ivory Coast, a year later before the devolution of military authority began to take place. With eleven of her former African colonies, France also made bilateral defence agreements which have tended to consolidate the military link at a time when it might have been broken.

The armies of Africa today are, therefore, the direct descendants of the colonial forces raised in their territories by imperial rulers. They differ primarily because of the differing attitudes of the particular European powers concerned. British and French military arrangements were characteristic of their own forms of colonialism: they both provided equipment, military training, and incidentally a tradition, but the degree of identification with the parent imperial army which they encouraged was markedly different. Only in a few cases has the chain of evolution from colonial to national institution been broken or damaged. In Guinea, Communist aid to fill the vacuum created by the French evacuation has left its mark on the Army; in Tanzania the mutiny of 1964 and President Nyerere's unique concept of African socialism have changed the character of the armed forces there; the disintegration of the 'Force Publique' in 1960 left the Congolese Government no alternative to the reconstitution of its army in a new mould. Generally, however, the Western type army has survived in Africa, but this has been patently no guarantee that the political behaviour of such armies would conform to any recognizable norm. At the same time it cannot be denied that imperial policies with regard to recruitment and Africanization have determined to a considerable extent their composition and that this has been a factor influencing status and attitudes.

II · The Social Structure of African Armies

The important elements in the composition of African forces are generally the ethnic and tribal proportions among all ranks, the different levels of education, and, among officers, significant groupings distinct by reason of age, rank, and experience or by training. Both the British and French authorities in Africa can be said to have applied, until the 1950s, essentially imperial criteria to the problem of recruitment. They operated on the basis of a combination of principle and expediency which was related to past experience in other parts of the world and to their own needs as administrators and agents of law and order within the colonial territories.

In British Africa men like Lugard naturally drew heavily on their Indian experience to the extent of employing cadres of Indian non-commissioned officers and skilled tradesmen. In East and Central Africa army units were actually created out of Sikh volunteers who remained in the area until as late as 1911. Paradoxically the original 5th Battalion of the King's African Rifles was actually an Indian unit sent from India to help deal with a mutiny of Sudanese troops in Uganda in September 1897. Ten years later there was still a mixed Indian and African unit in British East Africa. This policy, however, fell away as its costs and unpopularity with the Indian Government rose.

Early in the present century British recruitment policies in African territories fell into a pattern, influenced by Indian experience, which was only disturbed or readjusted during times of local crisis. The concept of the warrior type or of the martial race, of whom ready loyalty to the imperial command could be expected, was entrenched: the ideal soldier was generally supposed to be an illiterate, uncontaminated by mission education, from a remote area. Eventually to meet more skilled requirements this stereotype was occasionally modified, but always with reluctance. Basically it involved no more than the assumptions that an upbringing in the wild hinterland would have inculcated both physical toughness and political unconsciousness and that the countryman was always likely to make a better soldier than the town dweller. These notions were so deeply embedded in military thinking even within the British Army itself that they are scarcely worth questioning in the current context. It is only gradually, as war has become infinitely more sophisticated, that the military intellectual has found acceptance.

In the colonial situation the preference for warrior tribesmen from isolated regions was completely comprehensible. They had little in common with the coastal peoples and were capable of impartial, even hostile, action when serious internal security problems arose. Like their French counterparts the British, wherever they served, seemed to prefer the Muslim to the animist, the pagan, or the Christian convert, with profound consequences for countries like Nigeria. The regard of the expatriate army officer for his Hausa soldiers in West Africa was matched only by the affection of his civilian counterparts for the local rulers for whom they worked in Northern Nigeria, for instance. For years Islamic resistance to Western education was accepted as a fact of life with serious consequences in the shape of retarded development: nor did the encouragement of Hausa – as of Swahili in East Africa – as the language of military communication do anything to help educational and technological progress. In Nigeria these factors contributed heavily to the different rates of progress of the regions and thereby heightened intertribal tension and interregional rivalry.

B

Until after the Second World War the Nigerian battalions of the R.W.A.F.F. were recruited largely from Hausa speakers, many of them from the French territories across the northern border. In 1950 almost 80 per cent. of all soldiers came from the area north of the confluence of the Niger and Benue rivers, though most headquarters personnel and tradesmen were Ibos. The desirability of a conscious ethnic balance came to be accepted and a quota system of recruitment was adopted. This began gradually, as old soldiers retired, to alter the proportions in favour of the Ibos and the Yorubas. In the other rank context, where the initial numerical advantage was theirs, the Northern leaders saw the advantages of an eventually stable situation which also recommended itself to many expatriate advisers. Ibos, like the then Major Aguiyi-Ironsi, argued strongly in favour of enlistment in accordance with educational qualifications on the grounds that the federal public services of a united Nigeria should recruit on merit alone and take no account of origin. The quota system, strongly advocated by the British, was maintained on the basis of 50 per cent. recruits from the North and 25 per cent. each from the two existing Southern regions. Such quotas were undoubtedly responsible for the heated controversies which subsequently ensued over the accuracy of the census with its implication of readjustment should entirely new figures be revealed. Precautions were taken to ensure that recruits were not only resident in a region but that they and their fathers were native to it. In spite, however, of attempts to make provincial allocations in the North the Middle Belt, and the Tiv region in particular, came eventually to be over-represented in the Federal Army.

This method of trying to create and maintain a regional balance served the imperial purpose while tending to protect the interests of the North, especially when the earlier Hausa predominance was taken into account. The argument that an artificial ethnic balance was essentially against the interest of a modern state was countered by the claim that the enlistment of a high proportion of illiterates and phased procedure for discharge, some serving as little as six years, would assist the spread of education. In this way was the other rank composition of the Army of independent Nigeria determined by an interaction of imperial and specific local interests.

The relatively small size and comparative homogeneity of the Gold Coast encouraged a less formal approach to the problems of recruiting for the local regiment of the R.W.A.F.F. Like its Nigerian counterpart it was traditionally recruited from Northern, mostly Muslim illiterates, and even independent Ghana originally catered for a small proportion of French-speaking recruits. Four years after independence 60 per cent. of Ghana soldiers were from the Northern and Upper Regions in spite of their sparse population and the small proportion which it constituted of the country's total. Over the last twenty years the emphasis has shifted according to need from the North to Kumasi and the coast and back in a way which has tended to avoid the establishment of precedents and to minimize tensions. On occasions the encouragement of Northern volunteers for infantry service has been more deliberate than at other times and the majority of skilled specialists have been recruited in the towns on the coast. Recruiting officers up to 1961 were generally expatriates but these were not normally identified with any particular region. They, the politicians of the Nkrumah period and the present leaders, have seen virtues in a neutral force and for this and more general reasons the matter has never become a political issue. A comparison of the local circumstances in Ghana and Nigeria may suggest the extent to which expatriate prejudices and interests influenced the development of African armies, but it also indicates that the degree of expatriate commitment is affected by the nature of the particular situation. That this is so is largely confirmed by experience in other territories.

In Sierra Leone the declared objective was a tribal balance in the interest of stability but as in Ghana there was never a fixed quota. As a matter of convenience most recruits were found in Mende country on either side of the railway line to Bo but an effort, not always effective, was made to keep Mende strength down to about 40 per cent. of the total. An unusual feature of this particular situation was that most Mende recruits had had some years of secondary education in an area where educational provision almost outstripped demand. Mende–Temne rivalry and the aversion of Freetown Creoles from a military career tended to reinforce and consolidate the position of the major tribe. It is not perhaps surprising that the National Reformation Council after the military coup in 1966 found it necessary elaborately to balance tribal and provincial interests on that council and its committees.

In Kenya, Uganda, and Tanganyika the architects of the K.A.R. adopted a policy for recruitment essentially more discriminatory than that which was applied anywhere in West Africa. In East Africa tribes and ethnic groups were categorized according to a subjective assessment by the administration of their 'worthwhileness as soldiers' by which again was meant their martial qualities and reliability from a particular point of view. There was no attempt at representation in the armed forces proportional to population and indeed whole tribes, even the largest in a particular area, were excluded from the recruitment programme and, therefore, virtually unrepresented in the Army. In the event these, and, in particular, the Baganda and the Kikuyu, turned out to be those who profited most rapidly from the absorption of Western education, political ideas, and technical skills. In Kenya, admittedly, the necessary expedient of a total prohibition on Kikuyu enlistment during the Mau Mau emergency reinforced the existing trend, but it was certainly not wholly responsible for it. Not long before Kenyan independence the Army still consisted, to the extent of three quarters of its strength, of Kamba and men from the Nandi group of tribes. The comparative stability of the Kenya armed forces and the absence of extra-military action on their part, except for the mutiny of January 1964, must be attributed to the measures which the Kikuyu-dominated Government took to correct this situation and to inspire general confidence.

In Uganda, however, the bias towards Acholi soldiers has been an important factor in enabling the Obote Government to take stern action against Buganda and the other kingdoms, but it has also led to division in the armed forces which have brought the country from time to time to the brink of serious disturbance. It has certainly created doubts about its reliability in all situations and its discipline, particularly when dealing with foreigners. The Tanzanian situation is in striking contrast to this, in that there have been major difficulties in reconstituting the Army since the mutiny of 1964, but neither before or since have any of the problems been attributable to the tribal composition of the force. Tanzania is not so much homogeneous as composed of so many small tribes that significant vested interests do not exist. The ability of Tanzanians, excluding Zanzibaris, to think in national terms was surprising even in the months before independence and must be attributed substantially to the charismatic qualities of Julius Nyerere who by his characteristic actions in all fields has enabled such apparently unfortunate consequences of imperial policy as there were to be offset.

With regard to the Francophone countries of Africa, it is more difficult to be as precise about the effects of imperial recruitment policy, largely because the identification of units with particular territories was rare. Nevertheless it is not at all difficult to point to similarities between British and French attitudes to these problems. There was a typical bias in favour of soldiers from areas of the hinterland of Africa with supposed martial traditions. The emphasis on recruitment from these areas was reinforced by the resistance to conscription, and indeed drives for volunteer recruitment, which the French encountered from time to time in the Ivory Coast, Upper

Volta, and Dahomey. There were not infrequent cases of able-bodied males fleeing to the Gold Coast and Nigeria in order to avoid service. Such experiences encouraged the French to concentrate their efforts in, for example, the Sara Country of Central Africa, from which at times a very high proportion of recruits were drawn. As it happens these were not generally Muslims, whom otherwise the French like the British preferred, and this stood the French in good stead in North Africa and at Suez. There were cases of French officers deliberately encouraging the spread of Islam both on the grounds that its adherents made more reliable soldiers than others and that the 'superior' nature of the religion made it more likely that believers would be susceptible to the absorption of Gallic culture. On the whole, however, the fact that African soldiers were absorbed essentially into the French Army tended to lessen the importance of earlier recruiting policy for the newly independent states. It is important, however, to bear in mind the way in which *ad hoc* decisions based on imperial expediency inevitably established a structure which the new leaders of Africa had perforce to adapt to their own requirements. In that, however, military coups generally originate with officer corps, the nature of these elements in the national leadership élites is necessarily more important than that of the bodies which they lead.

Africanization of African Officer Corps

British colonial policy, loosely defined as trusteeship, envisaged the slow separate development of colonial dependencies to a point in the distant future when they might be able to stand on their own feet. British administrators saw, and in this they had the original experience with Canada and Australia to go on, responsibility for foreign policy and defence as the very last stage in the progress of a Commonwealth country to independence. Until Indian independence had been achieved they did not contemplate the type of comprehensive 'instant' freedom which was soon to become conventional. It was natural, therefore, especially in view of the slow spread of education in Africa, to give the commissioning of African officers a low priority. French acceptance of Africans as potential full French citizens facilitated a somewhat different approach to particular problems in their territories. If African leaders could acquire official political experience in Paris then the promotion of Africans to key posts in the public services followed. This did not mean, however, complete Africanization at an early stage. In fact, in 1948 the French Government was accused of putting deliberate obstacles in the way of Africanization and at that stage in Equatorial Africa only six out of 321 commissioned officers were Africans, and correspondingly in West Africa the figure was no more than 2 per cent., though in a somewhat larger force. The essential difference between the French and the British approach came later. In 1955 and 1956, the French tackled the problem on a massive scale by instituting preparatory military schools in West Africa and an African Officer Training School (L'Ecole General Leclerc) in Tchad. By 1960 their belief in the absorptive capacity of French civilization had transformed the situation while the British were still proceeding very cautiously and required higher initial standards of education and more thorough basic training.

In the same way as the valuable service of Africans with the Free French Forces in the Second World War had enhanced respect for them as soldiers and encouraged their advancement, men from British West Africa fighting in East Africa and Burma began to establish their position. Some became platoon commanders, but before 1947 only one achieved officer status. Whereas in India the essentially non-violent Congress party pressed vigorously in the early 1920s for the commissioning of Indian officers, the emerging political leaders in Africa after 1945 did not appear to give the question much consideration. The initiative then, and for years afterwards, towards the

Africanization of the officer corps came from expatriates. Local commanders backed by the War Office in London began to devise schemes which would gradually lead to a measure of localization. There was no urgency in the approach and no real pressures from educated Africans who had seen ample outlets for their talents elsewhere in more lucrative fields. The process of selection was essentially British in pattern and manned by Britons: it was rigorous and by definition culturally biased. Only the growing number of secondary boarding schools largely staffed by British teachers in West Africa enabled the officers on the selection boards to find any young men in their own image. Given the criteria built in to such a system progress was bound to be slow. On the whole it produced a high quality of officer, but in the end quantity was to prove as important. Other limiting factors were the unwillingness of the British to admit more than a small percentage of overseas cadets to their training schools on the grounds that there were dangers, first expressed with regard to Indians in 1922, of diluting the cultural heritage, and the caution of African politicians who saw political dangers in rapid localization.

The prospect of self-government for the Gold Coast, which began to loom in sight in 1947, raised the question of the provision of African officers for the R.W.A.F.F. as a serious issue. During the period between 1947 and 1951 the future commanders of the Ghana armed forces were commissioned. Among the earliest of these were S. J. A. Otu and J. A. Ankrah (Chairman of the National Liberation Council from February 1966), N. A. Aferi (Chief of Defence Staff at the time of the Coup) and D. A. Hansen who has commanded the navy. Almost all these and their contemporaries were serving in the education service, the only source of literate soldiers. These were often men from well-known families, educated at Achimota school or in an only slightly less reputable establishment and likely to be on good terms with their counterparts in the civil élite.

The advent of Nkrumah's Government in 1951 led to a gain-ing of momentum for the process of Africanization. The im-mediate potentialities for virtually direct commissioning having been exhausted, a more systematic mode of selection and train-ing became established, leading through elementary training schools in West Africa to Britain and the Royal Military Academy, Sandhurst, and also the two short service training schools at Aldershot and Eaton Hall, near Chester. Among those who were trained in the early stages of these schemes were Major-General C. M. Barwah who, having been an outstanding success at Sandhurst, was killed in the February 1966 coup, and Major-General E. K. Kotoka, architect of that event and subsequently assassinated in the attempted counter-coup. Kotoka was in some ways typical of the more mature cadets who received a shorter training. The regular process once initiated gradually accelerated and developed: further training at company commanders schools, on staff college courses and even at the Imperial Defence College followed naturally. By 1960 the distribution of officers of reasonable seniority was such that keyposts up to battalion commander and then Brigadier could be filled in the U.N. force in the Congo by Africans. Though the sudden replacement in September 1961 of expatriates in executive authority was a shock, the Ghana Army's own officer corps was not ill prepared for the ensuing responsibility.

The course of events in Nigeria resembled that in Ghana to a considerable extent. The first officers came from the same sources as those in Ghana – either the education service or from among the few who had achieved warrant officer status during or after the Second World War. Major-General Ironsi was one of these. The first two cadets to go to Sandhurst were ironically of Northern region origin; one became a brigadier after having been U.N. liaison officer in the Congo. Most of the early intakes were, however, Ibos from the heartland across the Niger beyond Onitsha. The plentiful supply of good secondary schools, like

Government College, Umuahia, in this area ensured that, given an open method of selection by educational merit and an only incipient military interest among the Northern élite, three quarters of all African officers in 1960 were Ibos. This portentous result was not curbed until considerably after independence by the adoption of a quota system. At the commissioned officer level the degree of individual western acculturation was clearly a decisive factor in selection. Education was preferred to more obvious martial qualities: in this way men could more easily be absorbed into the higher strata of an élite tradition. There were some who thought political neutrality would necessarily result from officer and other-rank bodies of essentially different tribal composition, but they were in the event proved wrong: one result is a Nigerian federal force weak in hierarchy because of the secession of Biafra. The accident of initial Ibo predominance produced a spiral of mutual suspicion between the Northern rulers, especially the Sardauna of Sokoto, and the Eastern élite, culminating in and substantially responsible for the disintegration of 1966–7.

Both Ghana and Nigeria by independence had Africans emerging in senior positions. In East Africa events and their timing produced a much less satisfactory result which fortunately did not rival in its consequences the Congo disaster of the Force Publique. It is not necessary to attempt to apportion the blame for this. Reforms were admittedly slow, but they were inevitably restricted by the relative educational backwardness of the whole region. Another limiting factor was the prevailing optimism in Kenya up to 1961 about the possibility of a multiracial state. This led to serious consideration both there and in Tanganyika of non-African, i.e. European and Asian, candidates for commissioning. Whether this would ever have arisen if there had been adequate educated Africans forthcoming is a moot point. The demands on the limited resources available were in fact so great there was in the end no alternative to the fairly large-scale commissioning of senior other ranks with long service. These had not necessarily any serious educational attainment and they and their wives were difficult to absorb socially in an élite service. Though they were plainly not of the background or calibre of their counterparts on the West Coast they more or less effectively filled a desperate need and Kenya even managed an African lieutenant-colonel as battalion commander by the time independence was celebrated in December 1963.

The mutiny in Tanganyika was, as will become evident, not unrelated to that country's failure to match the Kenya achievement. The dangers of officer-less armies were learnt more quickly in some areas than others. The composition and seniority of the transferred officer corps has proved of paramount importance to the development of African states.

III · Political and Social Adaptation

The conversion of colonial defence forces into national armies has unsurprisingly proved to be a process abounding in inherent difficulties. Even if those forces had been deliberately disbanded and new ones raised in their place there would have been no complete escape from the inheritance. The most important facts concerning this are the most simple and obvious – namely, that defence forces are necessarily instruments of law and order, closely identified with the administration and the original administration was, of course, imperial. Thus institutions, part of whose rôle has been to control violent political agitation, in due course, become the agents of the nationalist political agitators when they achieve power and might have to take action against a new type of political dissent. The strains and tensions involved in this transformation have rarely been faced up to: the assumption that defence and security forces would simply transfer their allegiance from one government to another has prevailed. Though the circumstances in English- and French-speaking Africa are different, this tacit assumption has generally proved to be justified in both areas. It is not possible to determine the extent to which a peaceful and orderly transfer of power has been the main ingredient in the apparent success, but it must be of considerable significance. At the same time the Western concept of the unquestioned obedience of an army to its political masters is clearly not to be altogether discounted as an influence even though the precept may subsequently have come to be disregarded. It is an impressive tribute to the effect of tradition that on the whole those armies of Africa, whose rôle in the achievement of independence was nil or minimal, so readily accepted the independence situation in its early stages.

The continuance of expatriate officers in key advisory and executive positions was, of course, a very important factor not only in the maintenance of continuity. Their very presence was a ready-made deterrent to unconstitutional action of any kind. They were also likely to provide a scapegoat when African officers felt that they had grounds for grievance. Again it is speculative the extent to which this may have been a useful safety-valve through which for a few months or years inter-tribal or other tensions were partially discharged. Nevertheless the existence of these foreign officers was also a check on the acculturation of the force in which they served. Experience has shown that in spite of the undoubted interracial tensions in forces like the Nigerian the retention of expatriate assistance tended to consolidate the professional tradition in the appropriate mould. Though it is unlikely that African armies will follow their Indian and Pakistani counterparts in becoming in some sense more British than the British, it is by no means certain that the trend towards the establishment of a particular professional pattern can be readily reversed. To an even less extent than with the other political and social institutions can the armed forces of most of the emergent countries of Africa be said to be truly national.

This situation is due to a number of associated factors. The nature of imperial rule is one, but probably more significant were the lack of a positive attitude on the part of most African politicians and the nature of the military life itself. There is not a great deal to be said about the former. The cultured African Frenchmen of the Francophone countries were not drawn into the ambit of the armed forces. Their interests were wide and there was little reason to think of defence as other than a metropolitan matter. Occasionally the matter of the provision of African officers assumed a certain urgency, but it was seen, if not as an academic problem, certainly as a symbol of native advancement rather than as important in itself. There is really nothing remarkable about this detachment: even in developed countries the armed services remain generally a matter of mystery or suspicion to almost all the elected representatives of the people. Where there are many other more humane concerns, provision for war takes a low priority unless to some extent it is seen as a means to the achievement of power. It is ironic that of all the first generation leaders of independent Africa only Julius Nyerere seemed to sense the importance of identifying the Army with the transition through independence. Before it was achieved his initiative and that of the then Governor led to him 'getting to know' the Army through the officers' mess and taking the salute on ceremonial occasions, but his knowledge in the event proved insufficiently intimate. Similar endeavours were made by expatriates in Kenya to interest the African leaders in their future army, but they only achieved success on a superficial level.

The present writer believes it to be no coincidence that only in Nigeria of the British administered territories were there signs of a closer military concern. At different times leaders representative of the three original regions gave vent to views suggesting their appreciation of the relationship of military to political power. Dr Azikiwe as early as 1949 referred in speeches to 'the martial glory of the Ibo race' – a phrase which was interpreted in an aggressive sense by his opponents. Chief Awolowo ten years later wrote in his autobiography of the dangers of the enlarged armed forces and of the purposes for which they might come to be used: he pointed to a Latin American example of what he feared might happen. From the North, traditional leaders who had often appeared to rate the Army as a career unsuitable for the proud Fulani, saw the rise of an essentially Ibo officer corps and openly endeavoured to redress the balance, eventually arguing bitterly about the location of training schools for the Army and Air Force. This in some senses unhealthy interest in things military was not

confined to the upper echelons of Nigerian society. Quite
junior civil officials were by independence willing to express
views on the place of the Army in society, and university and
college students actually asked for the opportunity of military
training in cadet corps. It would not be unreasonable to deduce
that the Army was seen from the different standpoints as a
means by which the 'Gordian Knots' of political rivalry and
competition might be cut. On the other hand, it is as easy to
exaggerate their importance as it would be to read too much
into the President of Zambia's sending of his son to Sandhurst.
Nevertheless the Emir of Katsina's earlier decision to send his
second son, Hassan, to the same military academy was, on his
own admission, clearly a small, but now significant, contribution
towards safeguarding the political position of Northern Nigeria.

The creation of a national military institution has in new
African states then not been a matter for deliberate local
decision: active interest in the possibility, where it has been
in evidence, has not been primarily concerned to produce a well
integrated force calculated to meet the national need. The closed
nature of military society too has tended to prevent total
assimilation of the originally alien organism. Whereas officers
of the other public services live side by side with other citizens
of similar socio-economic class – and even that separates them
as an élite from the mass of the community – the Army in
particular lives to itself. It experiences not only the isolation
of the cantonment but that of the camp, within which social
and medical services are provided both for men and their
families. Wives and children, as well as the soldiers themselves,
tend, in Anglophone West Africa for instance, to be disciplined and organized. The practice of appointing a wife of a
senior soldier to be in authority in the married lines was not
uncommon. Thus, of all social institutions, it is easiest for the
Army to maintain its integrity. This particularly applies to
officer corps, who like their civil service and police counterparts,
have inherited a foreign way of life and standard of living.

IV · The Nature of the East African Mutinies 1964

Though the Sudan had had a military government since 1958, the Force Publique had mutinied in the Congo in 1960 and a military faction had, in seizing power in Togo, assassinated President Olympio in January 1963, it was not until the East African Army mutinies of January 1964 that the African military establishments came to be regarded as of serious political significance. Even though in December 1960 an army rising had come near to overthrowing the Emperor of Ethiopia, it was customary to think of African armies as being generally too small to disrupt the political pattern of a state. As it happened, the East African mutinies when they came were probably less directly political in origin than incidents involving the military in other parts of the African continent. It might indeed be said that the political potential of African armies came to be more fully appreciated largely because the Tanganyikan force either missed or did not want the opportunity to seize power which its actions on Monday, 20 January 1964 appeared to create.

The Tanganyika Army between independence in December 1961 and the mutiny consisted only of what had been about one and a half battalions of the King's African Rifles, not all the soldiers in which had been recruited in Tanganyika. The original regional approach to the East African forces meant that Kenyan personnel serving in the Tanganyika battalion were no rarity. Idealism and economic problems had originally led Julius Nyerere to think in terms of dispensing with an army altogether. As late as April 1961, a few months before in-

24

dependence, he was genuinely inclined to want to disband his share of the K.A.R. when the time came. Prudence, prestige considerations, and the Congo situation eventually led him back to a conventional position on this matter, though he also had some qualms about the political dangers of an army. What he inherited seemed, by African standards, to be in most ways a trouble-free force. The British policy of recruiting from tribes considered to be 'worthwhile as warriors' had created no serious problems in Tanganyika. In 1963 the Tanganyika authorities recruited two hundred and eighty soldiers from thirty-eight tribes: they had employed the same pattern of recruiting safari and indeed the same kind of recruiting officer as in the period of British rule. In almost every respect this was still a British oriented army. The fact that Tanganyika was composed of groups from a large number of small tribes was as important militarily as it had already proved politically. Half the army were probably either Hehe or Kuria with large infusions of Yao and Ngoni, but their predominance in this quarter was not politically significant in a country where the political leadership had had great success in developing national unity and consciousness.

During 1963 Oscar Kambona, Minister of External Affairs and Defence, had announced the establishment of an air force and some expansion of the Tanganyika Rifles, but in fact the Army estimates for the year 1963–4 were somewhat smaller than for the previous year. Kambona's ambitions for the armed forces were linked at the time with the alleged imminence of a violent struggle for control of southern Africa, especially Mozambique and the potential of the armed forces in an economic and social rôle. The influence of the Israeli personnel at this stage may have encouraged thinking of the second kind, though the direct applicability of Israeli models to African conditions is certainly open to question. The claim of a social rôle for the Army is often a useful pretext for its expansion for other purposes. In any case, Kambona's words

C

had by the end of 1963 resulted in little action. The number of soldiers recruited in that year showed a small increase on the previous year and there had been some minor adjustment of the entry qualifications to make this possible.

The outbreak of the mutiny in January 1964 may have been contributed to by some vague political unrest and quite possibly personal ministerial machinations of one kind or another, but its roots were grievances over pay and conditions. The most important was related to the allegedly slow rate of Africanization of the senior ranks. As in East Africa generally the recruitment of indigenous officers was not regarded as an urgent matter in Tanganyika until 1961. By then one Tanganyikan Asian and two Africans, in that order, had been commissioned from Sandhurst. The multiracial ideal had thus a brief influence on policy even though there were no Asian other ranks. An intensive tour of educational establishments by a young British officer to interest African secondary school leavers in a military career produced good results and a more regular but still minute flow of cadets to Sandhurst and Mons Officer Cadet School began, though the vacancies at the former academy were certainly fewer in numbers than was desirable.

In fact, by the end of 1963, thirty-five officers in the Tanganyika Army were Africans of whom about half were warrant officers who had been directly commissioned to meet the obvious deficiency: there were still twenty-nine British officers, including all those who were majors and above. There is some evidence that the slow rate of Africanization was due to a lack of urgency on the part of the Tanganyika Government itself. Nyerere had spoken in 1961 of a ten-year period to complete the process. During 1963 British officers drew up a plan to complete localization of the officer corps by the end of 1964: at the time of the mutiny it was still lying in the Government offices, though its specific provisions, such as the early promotion of three officers to major, would have been an answer to some of the grievances. The Africanization of the chairmanship of the Officer Selection Board during 1963 was so far from having accelerated the training process that only three out of forty-three applicants were selected by this means in that year. It is true that this as well as some slowing down of the process in the civil service may have been due partly to President Nyerere's courageously expressed support for the notion of appointment and promotion on merit regardless of race, and to this extent may be attributed to a laudable effort to sustain racial harmony.

The mutiny at Colito Barracks, Dar es Salaam on 20 January 1964 was not entirely unheralded. In March 1963 the Junior Leaders' Unit at Kahawa in Kenya which was intended to provide potential officers and N.C.O.s for the three English-speaking East African countries mutinied or went on strike. This unit consisted of one hundred and fifty boys of fifteen years of age upwards. There was evidence of political inter-ference in order to stir up resistance to the expatriates running the school. The strikers were addressed by the British Com-mander of the Tanganyika Army and the mutiny ended. Eighty-three of the boys were discharged, but, contrary to the advice of the Commander, the ringleaders were not court-martialled. This certainly had repercussions in the Tanganyika force where there seemed to have been some doubt about the rôle and intentions of the Minister responsible, Oscar Kambona. The question is whether he was attempting at this time to establish a privileged position for himself *vis-à-vis* the Army at the expense of discipline and undermining the authority of British officers.

The Kenya independence celebrations in December 1963 exacerbated matters in that an African lieutenant-colonel was to be seen on parade in Nairobi and at the same time the matter of a group of fifteen officers trained under special arrangements in Israel seems to have come to a head. There seems to have been general uneasiness about officer selection, delayed pro-motion, and pay. For some reason the Vice-President, Rashidi

Kawawa, who presided at an officer selection board on 6 January 1964, rejected[1] all the officer candidates nominated by the Minister of External Affairs and Defence. At the same time the allocation to army posts of the fifteen Africans trained in Israel as youth leaders was causing embarrassment at the Tanganyika Force headquarters because of their general unsuitability for the purpose. The attempted appointment of officers in this way at one and the same time contravened the conventions for recruitment by public advertisement and competition and also installed dissident elements in the 1st Battalion, Tanganyika Rifles. They may have stimulated false representations of obstruction to promotion by the British force commanders. Five, with whose services the Minister had agreed to dispense, were still at Colito barracks when the mutiny broke out. Relations between the Minister and the expatriate officers on secondment were poor, and there was even political hostility to the promotion of British-trained Tanganyikan officers. This accounts for the fact that when the mutiny took place a number of African officers were treated as though they were British officers. In this connection Kambona seems to have taken the view that it should not be the young well-educated officers who obtained key positions, but older soldiers promoted from the ranks after years of service. This is the only established African case of blatant exploitation by a politician of the difficult inter-generation problem which is a feature of the rank structure of many African armies.

The effect on this delicate situation of reports of secret deliveries of arms to Dar es Salaam and of the violent revolution in Zanzibar does not need to be spelt out. Arrangements to fly the Tanganyika Rifles to Zanzibar were cancelled, it is not known by whom, at a moment when President Nyerere had left the capital. At the same time three hundred mobile police were sent to the offshore island, which is incidentally actually within sight of Colito barracks, thus leaving the door wide open

[1] Judith Listowel, *The Making of Tanganyika*, London, 1956, p. 430.

to military intervention on the mainland. There may at this time have been some mutual inflammation of one another by soldiers and students arising from Nyerere's recently proclaimed attitude to Africanization.

In the early hours of 20 January 1964 an efficient rounding-up operation which had clearly been planned and kept sufficiently secret for weeks resulted in the detention of the majority of British and African officers in the barracks' guard room and the easy establishment by the mutineers of general control of Dar es Salaam. The key points in the city including the radio station, the cable and wireless office, and the Standard Bank were all seized and roadblocks manned to prevent movement in and out of the city. At Nachingwea up-country and at Tabora mutineers took over at the same time with varying degrees of violence. The initial mutiny seems to have been organized by about twenty men with an education sergeant at their head: at an early stage they offered command to the only graduate African officer who subsequently appeared to have been coerced into accepting the cap of the British battalion commander as symbol of authority. Any question of external advice and support is unproven. If any member of the Government was directly implicated then it is surprising that, when a genuine power vacuum had been created, a take-over was not effected: the same would be true if foreign subversion had been involved.

In Dar es Salaam as the mutineers moved in to the city the President, Julius Nyerere, and other ministers were alerted and, with the exception of Oscar Kambona, went into hiding. This decision on the President's part has been attributed as much to the need to work out a solution to the situation as to fear for personal safety. In fact, the mutineers seem to have reached State House about 2.30 a.m. under the leadership of their ringleader, Sergeant Hingo Ilogi. Eventually, having failed to discover the President, they presented demands to Kambona in the process of which it is said they were violent and threatened

to shoot him. Their demands seem exclusively to have concerned pay and conditions of service and the replacement of
British by African officers. For what it is worth, this is confirmed by the account given in the book allegedly written by
Field Marshal John Okello[1] who was in Dar es Salaam at the
time and writes of hearing during the night that 'The Tanganyika Army personnel are mutinying about their pay' and
who claims that the following day he addressed a group of
mutineers at the T.A.N.U. (Tanganyika African National
Union), building appealing to them to desist from mutiny and
make their legitimate claims for more pay in other ways. In
fact Kambona seems already to have negotiated about these
matters and to have agreed to replace the British officers and to
examine the claim of the mutineers that in terms of pay they
were in fact worse off since independence than they had been
before. Whatever were the details of the discussions, the outcome was clear: whether it was Kambona's decision or that of
the mutineers unilaterally, the British officers were released
from the guardroom and taken to the airport to be flown to
Nairobi. Until they and eventually their families were off the
scene there was clearly a danger that they would be illtreated or
used as hostages. At various times during the day individual
members of the Government and officials of the T.A.N.U.
party were detained by the mutineers and occasionally roughly
treated. More important, as the leaderless state of affairs
became apparent, rioting and looting broke out in the Arab
and Asian quarters of the city and at least seventeen people
were killed. Fortunately this anarchy seems to have been
shortlived partly because the remaining police force seemed
unwilling to co-operate with the mutineers. On the evening of
the first day Kambona broadcast to the nation a strictly
military and non-political interpretation of the events at
Colito barracks: the following night after minor disturbances

[1] Field Marshal John Okello, *Revolution in Zanzibar*, Nairobi, 1967, pp.
173–5.

during the day Nyerere emerged from hiding and appealed over the radio for calm.

On 22 January the President succeeded in calming the population by a tour of the city but failed to make progress in negotiating with the mutineers. He was certainly slow to realize the strength of their position and reluctant to involve the outside, that is to say British, military assistance which was now available to him on ships offshore. He were clearly in no position to condemn the mutineers because he could not take any effective action against them. The situation was transformed when information about a political attempt to exploit the circumstances of the mutiny began to filter through from Morogoro where certain subversive elements had met. Clearly a co-operative effort between the politically frustrated and the mutineers would prove irresistible to the Government. The mutineers were themselves becoming more intransigent and seemed about to renounce their own leaders. It may be that discontent was also spreading in the police force. For Nyerere the finally persuasive factor in inviting direct British assistance was undoubtedly the news that the Prime Ministers of Uganda and Kenya faced with similar situations were endeavouring to settle their mutinies by the use of British troops. A written request directed through diplomatic channels to the British Government led on the morning of 25 January 1964 to a remarkably efficient and almost bloodless operation by Royal Marine commandos from the carrier *Centaur*. The mutineers were rounded up and during the ensuing week union leaders, some policemen, and others were arrested. The majority of the mutinous soldiers were simply discharged and the fact that virtually the whole army had been involved would have left Nyerere's Government defenceless had it not been possible to obtain in the meantime the temporary help of a Nigerian battalion when the British withdrew.

The Tanganyika mutiny may thus be summed up as essentially domestic in character and concerned with grievances:

inevitably, however, it opened the doors to political exploitation. The problem was to replace the virtually disbanded army with reliable troops. Initially the response to appeals for recruits was poor: the President invited members of the T.A.N.U. Youth League to enlist. In this attempt to identify the politically minded youth with the security of the nation he was to some extent following the example of President Kenyatta who had sought to redress the tribal balance in his own army in this way. It was clear that no African Government could accept long-term reliance on foreign military assistance, but at the same time the Organization of African Unity proved quite unable to agree on raising any kind of international armed force to be available to its members in an emergency. Tanzania, with its southern provinces harbouring bases for the training of Southern African 'freedom fighters', had to act as host to experienced irregular soldiers from Algeria, Cuba, and elsewhere. In the circumstances, a reliable force of her own was clearly a necessity.

The mutiny in 1964 made the task of building a national military institution immeasurably more difficult, and the enlistment of youth wing personnel combined with the reported re-enlistment of some of the rank and file mutineers was not reassuring from the point of view of national stability. These problems have continually engaged the mind of President Nyerere. He has wanted to train an army not as an élite force but one fully integrated into the national life. In August 1964 he was at pains to justify the mixture of training arrangements in which the country was becoming involved and, in particular, the presence of a small Chinese contingent. Questioned[1] on the risks implicit in such a step, he responded, 'What are the risks that I am taking? The army that proved itself disloyal to my Government was not one that was trained by the Chinese. There is always some element of risk about having an army at all in a developing country, but since you can't do without

[1] *The Observer*, 30 August 1964.

an army in these times the task is to ensure that the officers and men are integrated into the Government and party so that they become no more of a risk than, say, the Civil Service.' The mutiny demonstrated that in some senses the process of Africanization is closely linked with the securing of a national consensus, but it has not yet been established whether Tanzania has successfully found a more stable formula for a new kind of national army, given an effective break with the colonial tradition, than its counterparts elsewhere in Africa. In August 1966, for instance, there were reports of disturbances at Mkuyuni Camp, about one hundred and twenty miles from Dar es Salaam. In the meantime officers for the Tanzanian force have continued to be trained in a number of countries including Britain.

Of the three countries affected by the 1964 army mutinies in East Africa, Kenya seems to have isolated and dealt with the incident most successfully. This may be attributed to a special determination on the part of the Government in the light of the threat to national integrity constituted by the Somali problem in the north-east. With the aid of British troops already available in the country the dissident elements of the 11th Battalion Kenya Rifles at Lanet barracks near Nakuru were soon arrested. About one hundred men were court-martialled and mostly severely punished, and another one hundred and seventy dismissed the service and a new unit formed which included members of the Youth Wing of K.A.N.U. (the Kenya African National Union). The relatively advanced state of Africanization of senior ranks and the small proportion of the Army involved enabled the Kenya Government fairly readily to ride out the storm. The extent to which the incident was simply imitative of the Tanganyikan mutiny is, of course, impossible to assess: on the whole the Kenya forces had less to complain of in terms of pay and advancement. There certainly seems to have been less embarrassment, than in Tanzania, on the part of the Government in Kenya in calling for British assistance: this was, publicly at any rate, regarded by President Kenyatta as a natural device to meet a difficulty.

The links between Kenya and Britain have been retained on both the training and operational planes in spite of at one time frequent reports of young Kenyans training in Eastern Europe, in particular Bulgaria, and the fact admitted by President Kenyatta that even before independence Air Force trainees had been sent to Israel. By such a pragmatic approach the Government of Kenya managed in the years following independence to maintain progress and morale, and the dangers of tribal rivalry, which some thought great before, on the whole tended to diminish. As in Nigeria, however, the Kenyan Army would, if such tensions were to grow, be likely to magnify them and become the scene of their expression in a violent form rather than of their control and restraint.

In Uganda to some extent this has been true: an Acholi-dominated army at independence clearly needed a greater representation of Baganda and other major tribes throughout its ranks. The officer corps was weak in Africans: the overall situation was like that in Tanzania but potentially more explosive because of the clash between the Prime Minister and the Kabaka. Like the other two East African countries Uganda inherited its army from the King's African Rifles: there was at independence in October 1962 only one battalion of Uganda Rifles, in total less than one thousand men, stationed at the Jinja barracks overlooking the Owen Falls Dam. This battalion had seen a good deal of service not only in Kenya during the Mau Mau emergency but all round the frontiers of Uganda.

In the north-east there was a long history of intertribal difficulties and of raids backwards and forwards across the frontier with Kenya. A chronic problem with refugees from the Sudan demanded vigilance in that area and from 1960 onwards the border with the Congo had to be manned and there had been continuous incidents involving Congolese forces, including a situation in which wounded soldiers were finding their way to a hospital in Uganda. It was inevitable in these circumstances that some expansion of the army should be contemplated so that, in particular, a permanent detachment could be maintained in the Karamoja area. This did not represent any problem from the point of view of the recruitment of rank and file. As in most African countries, regular pay, food, and accommodation were an adequate attraction, and there was also to a more marked degree than in any comparable country a surplus of reasonably educated middle-school leavers. The fairly extensive provision of good education facilities especially by the missions in Uganda should have meant also that the raising of officers would not be difficult either. There had, however, been many difficulties in finding recruits willing to undergo what was seen as an arduous training and as late as 1961 there had been talk of bringing back the one Ugandan cadet from Sandhurst temporarily for a publicity campaign.

At the time of independence in 1962 there were precisely nine Ugandan officers in the army, all commissioned in the preceding eighteen months and, with one exception, directly from senior serving soldiers. There were at that time twelve more in training or on their way to training in Britain. In a sensitive political situation of the kind which quickly developed in Uganda between the Central Government and the kingdoms this amounted to a delicate problem. This may well have accounted for the rapidly changing mood of the Army which observers noticed after independence. Whereas at the time of the general election in March 1961 it was generally felt that the majority of soldiers were disinterested in politics in spite of persuasion to register, to attend public meetings, and to vote; eighteen months or so later political difficulties of an interracial character were rife. To emphasize the racial character of developments would seem to some who have admired the

comparative racial harmony of the Ugandan community
unfortunate. It is, however, a fact that from independence
onwards the Army's problems centred round pay differentials
and alleged misdemeanours towards Africans by British
personnel and that the Ugandan Army in recent times has not
been notably gentle with Europeans during periods of political
tension. The situation was not assisted by the mode of handling
grievances in the early stages. A decision to get a Minister to
explain to the African soldiers the standing of the British
personnel *vis-à-vis* his government had its merits, but in the
event the effect was to establish a practice of complaints from
the ranks directly to leading politicians about the conduct of
officers. This unsatisfactory state of affairs was exacerbated
by the involvement of two ministers, whose attitudes did not
always coincide, in the affairs of the Army and by the fact that
one of them insisted on talking to the Ugandan officers
separately from their British colleagues. From an early stage
after independence there was a deterioration in relationships
between the two groups in the same officers' mess. Unfortunately the decision to expand the Ugandan Army was not accompanied by the rapid construction of the necessary facilities
and at the same time as tensions mounted for political reasons
there were grounds for grievance about poor accommodation at
Jinja.

A further complication of a delicate situation lay in the
fact that a proposed reorganization of the Army command in
1963 did not immediately lead to a separation of that function
from that of the day-to-day administration of the main unit.
Instead of creating a bond of unity on the basis of common
training the return of the first substantial group of Ugandan
cadets from Aldershot brought about a deeper mistrust between
African and British officers. Whereas in other countries the
core of the difficulty had lain with the older officers who were
not able with their families easily to adjust to new social
conditions, in Uganda it was the young men who were the focus

of disaffection. The failure gradually to lay the foundations of a professional officer corps before independence and then the attempt to do it almost *en masse* afterwards explain the intensity of Uganda's difficulties in this respect. From mid 1963 it was clear that trouble was brewing and the extent to which officers were the instigators of other rank discontent can only be surmised. Two incidents that year showed clearly the trend of events: on one occasion the most junior officer asked that the senior British officers be required to leave a meeting of the regimental officers with a Minister and about a month later there was a substantial refusal to obey an order given by a British warrant officer, but unfortunately there were not adequate grounds for the offenders then to be dismissed the service.

As in the case of Tanzania where the effective pay of soldiers had appeared to fall since independence, so in Uganda there was anomaly in the relationship of the scales of the newly commissioned African officers and those for the senior other ranks. An attempt such as that which had been made much earlier in Ghana to rationalize the pay of men in all the security services was put in train, but in the event the importance of this particular demand was not recognized by the Uganda Government. In spite of direct representations to a Minister, it was clear by the end of December that the Government regarded army pay as having a relatively low priority. This was a reflection of a typical lack of appreciation by African politicians of their armed forces which long after independence they tend to see as relics of imperialism and not really their own: in the Uganda case it might have proved disastrous to the new state without, ironically, the assistance of British troops. Again the situation was exacerbated by a degree of political ineptitude in handling the impending crisis.

The Tanganyika mutiny and rumoured reports of its success in achieving satisfaction of the soldiers' demands naturally

inflamed passions in Uganda and a ministerial announcement
of an interim pay increase for the higher grades of other rank
only accompanied by a vague promise of a review for the rest
proved the last straw. On 23 January 1964 the opening scenes
of the mutiny were enacted: at this stage the hostility of the
soldiers was clearly directed towards the politician who seemed
to have failed them. They did not, however, seize the clear
opportunity of arming themselves, but they did take steps to
prevent police intervention. For a time British and African
officers were united in attempting to restrain the mutinous
men. The Minister of Internal Affairs in due course arrived
once again at the camp and was immediately coerced into
signing a document authorizing a massive pay rise which the
soldiers demanded should be implemented at once. While
this was going on the Prime Minister some seventy miles away
had apparently authorized intervention by British troops, a
measure which the visiting minister tried to claim was unnecessary. By the evening a battalion of British troops from
Kenya was established at Entebbe Airport.

The following day, 24 January, there was some activity
among the troops and a visit from another minister who
seems to have faced a demand for the removal of British
personnel and to have himself been inclined to attribute some
of the discontent to the attitude of his colleague who had visited
the camp previously. During the evening, however, the possibility of a seizure of arms from the armoury mounted and
only the persuasive powers of Major Amin, later Deputy
Commander of the Uganda Army, caused the groups of malcontents to disperse. During the night British troops arrived to
seal off the camp, arrest the ringleaders, and secure the arms
and ammunition. Coincidentally Amin and another officer
obtained from the Prime Minister at Entebbe promises of
changes including the confirmation of the promised pay-rise
and immediate Africanization of key posts. Amin then returned
to Jinja as Commanding Officer and the withdrawal of certain

British officers and most of the families began. Within a day, however, he was faced with a situation in which it was clear that the militant mutineers were threatening those Ugandan soldiers who had attempted to control the ugly situation of previous days. This led to further action by British troops and the discharge of the men of the two companies concerned: the wisdom of this decision in the light of experience elsewhere in Africa could not be seriously contested. Thenceforward the political preference for officers of particular tribes and the uncertain position of the remaining British officers were difficulties enough, of which the latter was largely resolved by the removal of expatriates from all executive posts and the appointment of a few advisers.

The mutiny of the Uganda Army demonstrated clearly that in a newly independent state with political problems of a tribal nature there was little prospect of isolating even the best trained of armies from political influences. Inevitably the rash promises of nationalist leaders in the pre-independence period were reflected in demands for more pay. Natural ambition combined with the need for a scapegoat to focus some of the discontent on the rôle of British officers. The fact that they survived in executive capacities in any numbers for a far shorter time in East Africa than in Western Africa is clearly a reflection of the more hasty steps to Africanization which had to be taken in that area, as was the clash between the school leavers who had been commissioned via cadet training and officers directly commissioned from the ranks. The Uganda mutiny left scars in the Army and repeated reports of alleged conspiracy are the symptoms. Once an army has realized its strength in its own or in a political cause it becomes a potential danger to the established political order. In Uganda the normal stationing of main army contingents in remote regions, on the frontiers or at Jinja well away from the capital and the centre of administration, may turn out to be an important factor in the political development of the country. The East African mutinies as a whole emphasize the importance of special attention to the welfare of armed forces, whatever the inclinations of the politicians, and the advantages of even a slender degree of professionalism if there is an opportunity and time to cultivate it.

V · Examples from Francophone Africa

The East African armies, and their counterparts in former British West Africa, were up to three or four years after independence, still virtually the colonial defence forces of the area renamed. In French-speaking Africa the situation was different. Many Africans recruited in the different territories had in effect joined the French Army and were French soldiers. This complicated the situation at independence and accounts for the delay experienced in countries like the Ivory Coast in achieving the transfer of locally raised contingents to indigenous control. Heavy recruitment by the French authorities for service in Indo-China and North Africa moreover meant that there was generally a surplus of African soldiers to be discharged on to the local labour market at the critical moment. For this reason, ex-servicemen have in Francophone Africa played a much more definite rôle than in former British territories, where post-war demobilization created only a temporary problem and spur to political activity. Redundant manpower was not likely to contribute to the stability of generally rather small states whose economic viability and potential was in doubt. The sequence of events varied from country to country but the political and economic problems of former French West and Equatorial Africa have on several occasions been clearly linked to the military situation. One or two examples will serve to highlight the characteristics of this interaction.

In important respects Togo, as a United Nations Trust erritory, pioneered the route of Francophone countries to ndependence, for it was the activity of Sylvanus Olympio at the U.N. which tended to influence de Gaulle towards a policy of constitutional reform in Africa. His response to this influence proved a clear example of de Gaulle's shifts of policy on the basis of expediency: when he came to power in 1958 he had in fact been committed to preventing the infection of French territories by the growing movements to independence in the neighbouring British areas. In practice he instituted the referendum which led to independence for almost all French tropical African territories within two years and this in its turn made nearly inevitable a resolution of the Algerian problem along similar lines. The end of the Algerian war made redundant many African soldiers who were discharged in their own countries and introduced a new and disturbing factor into an already uncertain situation.

The tiny territory of Togo in January 1963 experienced the effects of the shockwave caused by demobilization and found this impossible to absorb successfully. Togo is, as it were, a thin sliver of the African landmass with a short coast line and defined by boundaries drawn as arbitrarily as those of any territory by the British, French, and Germans as colonial powers. It happens also to be the homeland of the Ewe people some of whom live in adjoining Eastern Ghana and are prominent in that country's affairs in the persons of men like Police Commissioner J. K. Harlley and K. A. Gbedemah: Ewes have also found their way as immigrants into the Civil Services and police forces of the Ivory Coast and Senegal and have a unique reputation in West Africa for the ability to develop technical skills. During the German colonization of the area they were the only Africans who were allowed to be taught in German and duly benefited from this favour. Their general energy, desire for progress, and undoubted sympathy for Western modes of education made it natural for them to volunteer in fairly large numbers for the French Army when it conducted intensive recruiting campaigns in neighbouring Dahomey. Following the disbandment of French African regiments after the Algerian settlement more than six hundred Togolese had to return to the Togo Republic. Hardened by years of service in Indo-China and North Africa they were a clear threat to the security of a small compact country of less than two million inhabitants. It is a fact that Guinea, whose relations with France at that time were somewhat different, actually refused to receive a demobilized contingent and sent them back to France. Organized by a sergeant named Emmanuel Bodjollé the Togolese group became a powerful pressure group working for the expansion of Togo's minute two company army, which had been handed over by the French in 1961, so that they themselves could be absorbed in military employment. The French military adviser to President Olympio also favoured a larger force for reasons of efficiency. Like one or two of the more thoughtful African politicians Olympio was not anxious to expand his defence forces, largely on the grounds of expense and his estimate of relative social priorities.

The military situation of Togo at this time was only in one sense precarious. Ewe irredentism fanned by Nkrumah created an uncertain situation along the frontiers of the two countries and from time to time the frontiers were closed when it seemed that Nkrumah's imperialist inclinations might take practical shape. The risk of a Ghanaian invasion of Togo was never great, largely because both parties accepted that French intervention would quickly follow under the terms of the defence agreement which Olympio had made with France in 1960. There were also clear indications and even a personal assurance from the then Secretary General Dag Hammarskjold that U.N. intervention would follow such an invasion. Olympio had, moreover, a natural aversion from re-employing the professional soldiers because he suspected their political motives and regarded their rôle in the Algerian war as a betrayal of the cause of African independence. Though in the event he agreed to a relatively small increase in the size of his army he refused to allow the recruitment for this purpose of the discharged veterans and preferred to take unemployed school leavers off the streets. Within a few days of this decision a small number of the malcontents had staged a coup under the leadership of Bodjollé and the President himself had been killed, reputedly by the hand of Etienne Eyadema who eventually became head of the military Government.

As with most military coups the motivation was in a sense negative: the leaders had no precise policy or programme which they intended to follow. There was also the question as to whether the Ghanaian leadership had had a hand in it. Certainly the prompt appearance at the Ghana frontier of Antoine Méatchi, former leader of the Union Democratique des Populations Togolaises, and the revelations of the post-Nkrumah investigations in Ghana suggest that there was such a link. In the event Méatchi was beaten to the Presidency by Nicolas Grunitzky who had been in Dahomey and was regarded by President Maga as a suitable anti-Nkrumah figurehead for the ex-servicemen administration. The fact that Grunitzky had at one time been supported by the French as an opponent of Olympio made him the more acceptable, so Méatchi had to be content with the Vice-Presidency. The expansion of the army to twelve hundred men was, needless to say, first priority for the new Government: thus in a curious way the discharged veterans' coup led to a military government and one in which the Ewes from the south were at an apparent disadvantage, for almost all the leaders of the new administration were from the Kabre tribe in Northern Togo.

Generally speaking, however, the military junta in Togo behaved in a reasonably tolerant fashion. Certain Ewe exiles returned to the country and came to fill many posts of key responsibility in the ministries. In fact, their success in re-establishing themselves became a threat to the régime in that the political leaders dealt with them only through lesser personages who had no ability to control their activities and at the same time Olympio's party, the Unité Togolaise, was effectively resuscitated and was even represented in the cabinet. In January 1965, the junta was divided against itself to the extent of Bodjollé being displaced and imprisoned by Eyadema, when the real problem was the growing disaffection of the Ewes who were by now virtually indispensable in the Civil Service. Some of them favoured militant action, others more subtle penetration of the régime in power. In November 1966 the Unité Togolaise under the leadership of Noë Kutuklui attempted to seize power but, with only a small group of Ewe army officers on their side, the related demonstrations were easily and peacefully broken up. President Grunitzky evidently felt that this was an appropriate moment to move towards civilian rule, but he was inevitably resisted by Eyadema whose firm action merely confirmed that since Olympio's death real power had always ultimately rested with the group of northern army officers in the junta.

Nevertheless Togo's problems remained. Under Olympio's leadership the small country had carried weight in African affairs quite disproportionate to her size largely because of the President's unique standing as link-man between Francophone and Anglophone Africa. Under the Eyadema régime Togo became increasingly indebted to France and West Germany and really ceased to have international status. The degree of indebtedness was such that many of the Ewe élite saw the situation as a triumph for French 'neo-colonialism' and blamed the economic difficulties of the country on its military leaders on the grounds that economic development since 1963 had misfired. The outcome of five years of essentially military rule has been to provide a classic example of the dilemma of such a régime – a dilemma admittedly magnified by the tribal identification of the main groups involved. The possibility of return to civilian rule has always meant in Togo, in particular, the revival of the old political parties with the probability of a deadlock between that based in the north and that in the south, almost certainly resolved by some manipulation on the part of the administration. The circumstances of Olympio's death in 1963 and Ewe emotions on the subject certainly do not preclude the organization of judicial revenge which naturally is not an attractive proposition to those who might be held responsible. The fact remains that Togo has always been largely civilian-administered and that the original coup had only a short range objective but the military leaders would run personal risks in disengaging from ultimate responsibility.

There are other factors in the Togo situation making for the maintenance of the status quo. The Ewe link with the Ghanaian leadership and the tradition established by Olympio of an individualist rôle in West Africa, seeking close co-operation with Commonwealth countries, might be to Togo's economic advantage, but would not be popular with de Gaulle's France. The possibility of sharing, as was originally planned in the electricity production of the Volta Dam, might involve an unacceptable realignment of Togolese foreign policy. The military régime because of its training and origin serves to strengthen the links with the Organization Commune Africaine et Malgache (O.C.A.M.) and with France. The fears of the leadership for their personal security and French pressures may cause Eyadema to continue in office. But his position is very different from that of his military neighbours in Ghana. There the identification of the public service élite, civil, police, and military, with the régime of the National Liberation Council has been almost total and there is no fundamental tribal division. The position of a military administration is always such that it is likely in most circumstances to grow apart from the country which it serves. It is questionable how long such an authority can rule in opposition to the local meritocracy, but recognition of this danger would involve the overt revival of political parties with their past associations. The peculiar mode of the military's accession to power in Togo may be matched by the nature of its end: because of its exceptional features the Togolese example of a military coup provides useful pointers for the interpretation of others which may be thought more conventional.

In recent Togolese history the barely concealed hand of France has had influence upon domestic politics, but not in so marked a fashion as was the case in the more prosperous economy of Gabon in February 1964. On 17 February a newly formed revolutionary committee through the agency of about one hundred and fifty soldiers – approximately one-third of the country's total armed forces – under the leadership of two lieutenants, Mombo and Essene, attempted to seize power. The intention was to form a new government under M. Jean Hilaire Aubame, and M. Mba, the President, was, apparently at gunpoint, prevailed upon to resign in order to make this possible. The origins of this attempted coup were rooted farther back in Gabon history than others elsewhere appear to have been. M. Aubame was a former Foreign Minister, who had been three times elected a member of the French National Assembly and been the political opponent of the President, Leon Mba, for twenty years.

In 1957 M. Mba's party, the Gabonese Democratic and Socialist Union (U.D.S.G.), had actually had a majority at the elections but had been progressively eased out of influential political and official positions in the intervening period. During 1963 there had been an uneasy alliance between U.D.S.G. and Mba's party, the Gabonese Democratic Bloc (B.D.G.). The manipulation and political elimination of U.D.S.G. personalities had been viewed with disquiet and, at the time of the coup, elections were about to be held with the B.D.G. in the field on a one party basis. This was a clear case of a popular opposition leader acting as a focus for elements resisting an increasingly authoritarian government and securing the support of a substantial proportion of the armed forces. The attempt was evidently precipitated by President Mba's decision to dissolve the National Assembly and to purge the administration of U.D.S.G. and other opposition supporters. The causes of the coup were essentially political, for Gabon was then and remains for its size one of the most prosperous countries in Africa: its annual exports amounted in 1963 to $100 per head of the 500,000 population. It was able to balance its own budget and to have a balance of payments surplus: the principal contributory factors to this sound situation were oil, uranium, and one of the largest deposits of manganese in the world. Nor is it likely that the immediate French intervention on behalf of Mba was wholly economically inspired: the political explanation seems in retrospect to have been more valid.

President Mba was one of the most Francophile of African leaders. The French Government stake in the oil investment was heavy, but it is more likely that President de Gaulle did not feel he could afford to lose, by default, political support in Africa at a time when Britain had just demonstrated her ability to act in support of legitimate governments to suppress the East African mutinies. It was, however, by no means certain that the situation in Gabon was really parallel to that on the other side of the continent. The consolidation of an oppressive régime against what appeared to be legitimate opposition and the intention to hold a single list election might have been thought to invite popular displeasure. Whatever the reasons, the French action was rapid and, after some hours of doubt, effective. The defence agreement between Gabon and France was invoked through the Vice-President, who was three hundred miles away, probably at the instigation of the French Ambassador. French and French African troops from Dakar, Chad, and Congo (Brazzaville) were flown in while President Mba remained a hostage of the rebels in the forest. Resistance at the barracks lasted long enough to cause the French commander some anxiety. The justification for French initiative in invoking the defence pact and intervening, though it may or may not have had to do with the supply of uranium for the weapon production for the *force de frappe*, was politically slender.

This attempted coup in Gabon was comparable with those successfully carried out without interference elsewhere in Equatorial and West Africa in that it reflected current popular discontent with politicians. Only six months before, the situation in the capital of Gabon's neighbour Congo (Brazzaville) had been not dissimilar and three thousand French troops in the vicinity had allowed events to take their course. In the Congo Republic President Fulbert Youlou, who had been in office for the whole four years since independence, had negotiated with the trades unions a plan for single party government through a *Parti Unique* which was in process of formation. At the critical moment the Government had banned all political meetings until this party could be created: this ban was treated by the unions as a deprivation of popular rights under the United Nations Charter. This led to the exertion of pressures on the President by the Unions supported by the Army.

The long history of political activity by Africans in Brazzaville even under French colonial rule thus rebounded on an African leader who sought to establish a more authoritarian régime. Fulbert Youlou was required to resign the presidency and the Army, in the person of a captain who replaced the French lieutenant-colonel normally in command, took over temporarily until a provisional government could be formed. Political discontent of a fairly sophisticated nature was augmented by more elementary grievances. Corruption in the Government was reputed to be rife and there was much criticism of the high salaries paid to ministers: even Youlou's sacrifice in dismissing most of these was not, however, sufficient. Workers were reported[1] as chanting outside the Presidential palace 'We want bread'. This was a case of the poverty of the masses finding expression through the unions and the Army. The economy of Congo (Brazzaville) was largely parasitic on the misfortunes of Congo (Leopoldville): smuggling and shady commercial transactions had enriched a few merchants and

[1] *Daily Telegraph*, 16 August 1963.

ministers. The President's endeavours to attract investment had not been successful: foreign enterprises evidently regarded the country's apparent stability as illusory and its government's anti-communist stance as no great asset. Such development as had taken place had only served to separate the leaders from the masses. Government affluence and popular poverty provided a classic incentive for military intervention. The fact that discontent also had tribal focus arising from Youlou's political entrenchment of the Bakongo tribe and the violent suppression in 1959 of the Baketes and other minorities gave it additional edge and enabled the trades unions to act. In so far as it exacerbated the divorce of the élite from the masses it was significant not only for the Congo Republic.

The affair in Brazzaville was of transient interest as part of the phenomenon of the military in politics. In the Dahomeyan capital of Cotonou there has been a succession of military interventions since October 1963, the first of them initiated by the trades unions. Events from December 1967 onwards illuminate particularly clearly the main characteristics of such coups in African conditions. Before that time developments indicated clearly the increasing involvement of a reluctant army as the country proceeded from crisis to crisis. In October 1963 President Maga's government was overthrown by the trades unions on whose behalf General Soglo administered the country until general elections could be held in January of the following year and President Apithy could be appointed. In November 1965 Apithy was deposed by the Vice-President Justin Ahomadegbe who had the support of youth organizations and army officers. The following day the Army intervened and appointed the former speaker of the assembly, Congacou Tahirou, as President and a month later there was a full military take-over and General Soglo became Head of State. The Soglo régime lasted from December 1965 to 16 December 1967: during the last few months it had faced growing military unrest. There were tribal divisions – some of the dissident officers like Major Kouandeté and Captain Kerekou came from the northern hinterland. There was also a typical intergenerational problem: young officers regarded Soglo's avuncular administration as conservative and weak. Earlier in 1967 they had replaced the *Comité de Renovation Nationale,* a mixed civilian, clerical, and military body, with a *Comité Militaire de Vigilance* under the chairmanship of an officer from the central regions.

These manoeuvrings, however, were only symptoms of a deep malaise in the south of the country arising from its basic economic instability. The facts were that the Soglo Government's appeal for retrenchment and a return to the land held little appeal for southerners attracted away from agricultural projects in search of white collar employment in the towns, particularly Cotonou. An austerity programme which included a 25 per cent. wage cut by direct taxation caused a direct confrontation with the unions and intervention on the part of young officers to prevent a general strike. They – 'the young officers of the Dahomeyan Army' – were readily able to accuse Soglo and his ministers of megalomania and shirking their responsibilities. They set up a Military Revolutionary Committee to replace their own, earlier, military vigilance committee. The problems, however, remained the same: a small complacent and entrenched urban middle class and a growing mass of unemployed workers in the south contrasting with some improvement in living standards in the northern rural areas. Dahomey's problems in these respects are generally typical of the Francophone countries in the area where there have been military interventions or threats of them. Upper Volta, Niger, the Central African Republic as well as Congo (Brazzaville) all suffer from virtually intractable economic weaknesses arising from a shortage of natural resources. It is clear that in these circumstances disillusionment with politicians readily flourishes and certain that military régimes will be associated with austerity and from time to time deploy the threat of force against a resistant civil population. It is, for this reason, that the course of events in Dahomey in December 1967 which led to the emergence as Head of State of Colonel Alphonse Alley is especially significant. It is important that Alley is a soldier of the younger generation – that of Afrifa in Ghana or Gowon and Ojukwu in Nigeria – and not one of the first generation military father-figures like Ironsi or Ankrah.

The course of the Dahomey crisis as it developed[1] displayed the full range of characteristics which tend to encourage the firm establishment of army rule. On 8 December 1967 the union of primary school teachers declared a forty-eight hour strike in support of salary claims. The Soglo Government's response was to declare all trades union activity suspended on the grounds of the misuse of trade union rights. This action originated with the Military Vigilance Committe and amounted to a declaration that the strike was illegal. The school teachers in the event defied the ban and were supported by other workers seeking to obtain the withdrawal of the 25 per cent. tax on salaries which in various forms had operated since June 1965. The Government claimed that this resistance to essential government austerity measures was a step towards anarchy brought about by professional agitators and undermined their attempt to obtain more aid from France on the basis of the continuation of a stern policy of retrenchment. The strike spread to post and telecommunications workers but the Government still made some attempt to avoid a final showdown with the unions. By 12 December progress seemed to have been made towards some limited agreement and an attempt was made to call off the threatened general strike and to invite the strikers already out to return to work. The following day, however, the strike spread to the railways and airports were closed. At this stage Lieutenant-Colonel Alley,

[1] See, in particular, in *West Africa*, Nos. 2639 and 2640 of 30 December 1967 and 6 January 1968, 'Dahomey Diary' a characteristically thorough report.

the Army commander, took the initiative in speaking to union leaders and saying that he would act as the unions' spokesman before the Council of Ministers the following day. This met and agreed among other things to the withdrawal of the ban on union activities and the release of arrested union leaders. Two hundred troops were drafted in to Cotonou and Porto Novo. But the strike continued.

At this point there appears to have been a division between senior army officers possibly along tribal or regional lines. Commandant Maurice Kouandeté from the north refused to attend a meeting with Colonel Alley in protest against alleged appeasement of the unions. Alley had already resisted pressures to lead an overthrow of the Government. The following morning two parachute commando units, with whose establishment Alley had been closely associated, surrounded his house, as well as those of President Soglo, of the Minister of the Interior and of the chairman of the Military Vigilance Committee. The young officers, led by Kouandeté and Kerekou, officers from the Northern Somba tribe, claimed that the Government had been paralysed by corruption and the vigilance committee silenced. The economic and social situation had deteriorated, and, most significantly, according to a radio broadcast 'The peasant masses, who were constantly asked to make a greater effort, were wearing themselves out with work without seeing their lot improved or any change'. The Government were 'drunk with power' and had behaved 'like veritable potentates'. The same broadcast announced the establishment of a constitutional committee leading to a referendum and the free popular election of representatives and the establishment of institutions. The pledge to transfer power to popular political leaders at the moment of its seizure implied a considerable trust in the political commonsense of the Dahomeyan people which did not seem to correspond with the disgust expressed concerning union activities.

The provisional government which was established was notable for the refusal of Dr Zinsou, who had been a member of the Soglo Government, to serve. In the first place the Government met actually at the army camp near Cotonou and denied its regional roots or any foreign or internal political affiliation. Colonel Alley still apparently head of the Army was openly critical to journalists of the need to seize power and spoke of the possibilities which had existed for reforming the old system. The following day, however, he seems to have been under house arrest and General Soglo to have taken refuge in the French Embassy. The trades unions demanded a greater voice for organized labour and, in particular, the elimination of the political influence of France and America over the Dahomeyan Government. Protests against French neo-colonialism have, for obvious reasons, not generally been upheld by Francophone military régimes. At a meeting between the revolutionary committee and the trades unions the dilemma was clearly stated. The restoration of the 25 per cent. cut in wages combined with a refusal of French aid there would result in a budget deficit of nearly £4 m.: even the payment of civil servants for the current month was at stake because the money was not available in the treasury. The demands of the unions combined with the fragile financial position constituted a serious problem for the provisional administration which by 21 December was of such severity that it was clear that the revolutionary committee lacked sufficiently broadly based support to survive. Colonel A. A. Alley was, therefore, brought into the Government as Head of State while retaining command of the Army.

In a broadcast on 22 December to the nation Alley referred to the indivisibility of the Army as being 'the only organized force in the country, where political parties have so far been mere electoral movements. Twice already, *at the request of the people*, the Dahomey army has been obliged to assume power.' He promised a return to constitutional government and elections 'within a maximum period of six months, no matter the circumstances'. Thus Alley emerged as leader to resolve the tensions which had developed within an army attempting to function politically in a situation of grave economic difficulty. It was not enough to demonstrate that the Government and peasants were one, as Soglo's ministers had done by working beside them in the fields, nor to criticize a departure from that degree of commitment and austerity. The restlessness of the young educated élite within the Army itself needed the restraint of mature leadership capable of mediation with militant civil groups. In particular, the traditional military mistrust of trades unions required modification if the Dahomey economic crisis were not to deteriorate into paralysis and permanent deadlock resolvable only by a degree of force which had not recently been a feature of life in Cotonou or Porto Novo in spite of turbulence.

The dominance in the minds of Dahomeyan leaders of the economic problem led to a degree of urgency about the return to legality and to constitutional rule unparalleled elsewhere in Africa. Alley's acceptance of office towards the end of December 1967 was followed by announcement of a referendum on 31 March 1968 with a view to a return to civilian rule on 17 June. The referendum was to determine the validity of a constitution drawn up in February. The whole operation combined shrewd political appreciation with brisk military efficiency which many associated with the personal qualities of Colonel Alley. Alley typically represents the younger generation of fully French trained army officers in Africa: in other words he is strictly a professional and as such not particularly attracted to involvement in politics. He comes from Bassila near the border with Dahomey in what may be termed the north central region of the country. His father was a soldier in the French Army who in the 1930s was in charge of training the Togo police. Alley went at an early stage to the school for children of soldiers at Bingerville in the Ivory Coast and to a military secondary school in Dakar. He belongs strictly to the mobile West African élite, cosmopolitan in outlook, and served in Indo-China, Morocco, and Algeria within a short time of first joining the French Army. He became a paratrooper with all the associations which that rôle had in North Africa and subsequently established such a unit in Dahomey. He returned to independent Dahomey as a lieutenant.

Alley's first real introduction to political matters came with Soglo's in 1963. Riots in the main Dahomeyan towns forced the Army to intervene and briefly to put affairs again on the right track. Re-intervention by the Army two years later in November 1965 appeared to Alley and others in the same professional cast as simply a means of preventing bloodshed by separating Apithy and Ahomadegbe who seemed on the verge of leading their factions into collision with one another. A month later the inadequacy of such an approach was demonstrated when the Army had to take over full power. Nevertheless the function of reconciliation between groups clearly had a high priority in the minds of the military leadership. The political parties must be brought together in a sense of national purpose in order to avoid a decline into regionalism. The obvious comparison with Gowon in Nigeria was made in the journal *West Africa*[1]. The fact that Alley, like Gowon, came from a small tribe between the north and the south made him, with his professional record, a natural champion of national unity. His training gave him an almost puritanical concern with cleansing corruption and an inclination to resist Soglo's view that the Army having seized power should stay to see the development plan through.

It is not easy to assess the extent to which Alley having ended up in power himself then sought to proclaim his own political innocence by dissociating himself from the faults in Soglo's régime: it is perhaps fairest to judge by his actions in rapidly initiating the return to civilian rule at a speed unparalleled in Sierra Leone, where it ought to have been easier, or Ghana. Certainly Alley was able to avoid excessive entanglement in the decline of Soglo's administration by the facts of being away

[1] *West Africa* No. 2652, 30 March 1968, p. 365.

for a period on a course in Paris and of being able to devote himself almost exclusively to military affairs. Corruption and a return to legality had ceased to be regarded as urgent issues within a year of Soglo's assumption of power. Typically, but perhaps with less than justice, the President was seen to have become just another politician. In the end his tactlessness in handling army discontent may have been decisive in causing his overthrow, for the motivation of the strikes appeared to be running out by the time the coup took place on 17 December 1967. This illustrated very well the political inexperience of Soglo and the outcome perhaps the greater realism of Alley when faced with a non-military situation. For Kerekou and Kouandeté must at some point have realized the weakness of their own relatively inflexible position and taken account of the prestige value of Alley's authority and indeed the need to conciliate the French without whose very recent financial concessions to Soglo the task of reconstruction was bound to prove much greater. In fact the essential budget aid from Paris was denied and Alley's programme thereby became more difficult to fulfil.

Politically Alley tended from the first to see national unity in single party terms. It is arguable that this is a natural standpoint for the military trained mind. It may be too that the referendum of 31 March 1968 on the proposed constitution for civilian rule gave Dahomey's leaders food for thought, about their own political potential, for 92 per cent. of the votes cast were in favour. In some areas like Colonel Alley's home town, Bassila, the figure was 100 per cent. Clearly Dahomeyans are capable of political organization. Only a substantial period will tell whether the older politicians are so imbued with the political 'mores' of the French Fourth Republic that they are incapable of organizing periods of stable government. It was this which apparently caused the young officers to wish to ban Maga, Apithy, and Ahomadegbe from the Presidential contest under the new constitution. Such pressures upon Alley gave a

E

clear indication that the Dahomeyan Army no more than any
other in Africa has really succeeded in reconciling military
intervention with the revival of political life.

Once having attempted to 'cleanse' politics of its impurities
officers have found great difficulty in accepting again the –
from their point of view – imperfections of civilian rule. The
subsequent imposition of conditions for the return to full
political life resembles the struggle which colonial administrators once had in envisaging the transfer of power to their
successors. The fact is that military governments have tended
to have standards of particular kinds not obviously shared with
the rest of the community: this has often seemed to be the
biggest obstacle to the transfer of power back to civilian hands.
An example of this may be taken even from the first three
months of Colonel Alley's period of office in Dahomey. In
January 1968 a special Military Tribunal was set up to deal
with cases of embezzlement of public funds and bribery. At
the beginning of April its decisions were declared null and
void and a new body called the Military Correction Committee
was set up in its place to reconsider all the cases already heard
as well as new ones. Major Kouandeté gave as the reason for
this the unsatisfactory attitudes of some of the civilian
magistrates on the original tribunal which, he said, amounted
almost to obstruction. Contempt for the non-military and the
consistent adoption of a 'holier than thou' outlook is perhaps
the most serious general obstacle to demilitarization.

Coups in Francophone countries have generally had little
significance outside their own boundaries. In addition to those
described, not wholly dissimilar incidents, usually bloodless,
have taken place, for instance, in the Central African Republic
(C.A.R.) where Colonel Bokassa deposed President Dacko and
in Upper Volta where Colonel Lamizana overthrew President
Yaméogo. On occasion the French have given tacit support to
threatened governments and once in C.A.R. they provided direct
military assistance under the terms of a defence agreement

Most Francophone countries in Africa have still a degree of military as well as economic dependence on metropolitan France not paralleled in the Anglophone territories. The influence of these special relationships on the domestic affairs of such small – in economic and political terms – states clearly affects the nature of military intervention in politics. So does their general lack of real economic viability: there are usually economic factors in the conditions leading to military coups, but they are clearly not the same factors when Ghana, Nigeria, C.A.R., Dahomey, and Gabon are compared. The general disillusionment with politicians which prevails is well illustrated in ex-French Africa, as is the tendency of armies to adopt a superficially almost puritanical morality: the decree of the Upper Volta régime prohibiting 'drumplaying and lying about in the sun except on Sundays' is not without parallel elsewhere. The Francophone states have special problems because of the fundamental weakness which is often a function of their small size and particularly arbitrary boundaries, but they are not immune because of this from the kind of inter-tribal jealousies which have torn apart their vast neighbour Nigeria. In short, a country like Dahomey has more than intrinsic interest for observers of the military in politics, because in this respect it can claim to be an African microcosm.

VI · The Tragedy of Nigeria

The main problem in considering the case of Nigeria as an example of military intervention in politics is to decide where the activities of soldiers end and those of civilians begin. This is one way of stating the obvious fact that in the history of modern Nigeria there have been points at which the fate of the Army has determined the fate of the nation. These self-evident truths are, however, too general to be of real value. What the historian wants to know is the extent to which the Army was the focus or simply the magnified reflection of the fissions which have torn the federal independent state apart and at what point in time the developing situation acquired a kind of tragic inevitability.

It would not be true to say that, in the important decade or so of colonial rule preceding independence in 1960, the British administration of Nigeria paid particular attention to the development of the Army as a national federal institution. The other public services in Nigeria, whether at federal or regional level, were consciously planned, as was the police force. Considerable care was taken over the question of relationship between the regional and federal organizations. In the case of the police in Nigeria, the federal force was originally under the direction of the Prime Minister and the operational command of the Inspector-General. The Prime Minister presided over the Police Council on which sat ministers representative of the three regions and which determined matters of major policy, while an independent Police Service Commission was responsible for staffing and recruitment. Operationally the officer in command of a regional contingent could

appeal against the instructions of the regional government
directly to the Federal Prime Minister and the Governor-
General. Two regions also had local forces. Central training
schools were provided and recruitment was conducted nationally with a result comparable in terms of tribal composition
with that prevailing in the Army. Because, however, of the
distribution of the police force round the country in small
subunits and of the corresponding lack of any large concentration of men this was of less importance than was the case with
the Army. The Army, moreover, lacked on any formal basis
the influence of regional checks and balances on its control
and development: the holders of federal political power
technically at least controlled the armed forces without restraint. The almost idealistic assumption that the Army could
be regarded from the first as a national force was reinforced by
the fact of its derivation from a West African formation.
Though Headquarters West Africa Command was disbanded
in 1956, the training organization and general tradition of the
individual forces as they developed after that date had an
almost supranational quality.

The R.W.A.F.F. heritage suggested a degree of professionalism which created the illusion that its regiments when parcelled
out to new states would act as national melting pots. There is no
doubt that the essentially mercenary nature of imperial service
exaggerated the tendency to expect apolitical impartial behaviour from the soldiers so recruited. To a slight extent at
least the innocent trust of expatriates in the simple soldiers
who had served them loyally must bear a responsibility for the
Nigerian explosion. And yet, even before independence, and
certainly immediately after it, there were signs of an exceptional – by comparison with Ghana, Sierra Leone, or the East
African territories – awareness in Nigeria of the political
potentialities of the armed forces. Such awareness was not
confined to a particular tribal group, though the Northern
Fulani aristocracy because of their initial contempt for the

military vocation were slowest to show their understanding.

As early as 1948-9, Dr Azikiwe in nationalist speeches was
referring to 'the martial glories of the Ibo race' – a phrase
which was reasonably disregarded at the time as harmless
rhetoric and was in fact in itself probably no more than that.
Nevertheless such an emphasis, however unconscious, on a
little-known aspect of Ibo history, became more important
when seen in the context of later developments. There is no
doubt that the growing enthusiasm in the 1950s of able young
Easterners, especially Ibos from Onitsha and Umuahia and
their environs, for a career as army officers was to some extent
politically inspired. There was evidence of conversations
between leading politicians and young school leavers, some of
whom had already chosen other careers, which were decisive
in influencing their seeking training at Sandhurst.

Colonel Ojukwu himself has said that it was on the personal
advice of Dr Azikiwe that he, educated at a British public
school and a graduate of Oxford University, transferred from
the administrative to the military service. Dr Azikiwe's interest
in such developments was not only practical but theoretical:
it was common knowledge that when the University of Nigeria
at Nsukka, which was founded at his instigation, was being
rushed through the planning stage he wanted to establish at
the outset an Institute of Military Science. As serving officers,
Ibos like Ojukwu were active military thinkers. Ojukwu as a
captain at the Ministry of Defence in 1960-1 put forward a
considered plan for the establishment of a joint training school
on a military basis for cadets for all the public services.

It was also from Ibo students that there came the pressures
on university and college authorities for the establishment of
military cadet forces: such contingents were in being at one or
two of the branches of the Niger College of Arts, Science, and
Technology – that at Ibadan being particularly flourishing
Nevertheless the writer recalls the reluctance of the Ibo D

Kenneth Dike, Vice-Chancellor of Ibadan until the secession of Biafra, to encourage such an innovation in the university. Neither he nor the students were under any illusions about the reasons for their enthusiasm for such an activity: they were aware of the political potentiality of military training. There was also a caution on the Vice-Chancellor's part lest an armoury on the campus should on some occasion provide a temptation to violence for some purpose. It is ironic that this student agitation was at its height at the time when resentment against the Anglo-Nigerian defence agreement expressed itself in the form of an invasion by students of the Parliament building in Lagos – an action which was interpreted in some quarters as reflecting an essentially pacifist desire for non-involvement and non-alignment.

As has already been indicated the response of Northern leaders to the military problems of independence was rather tardy, but by 1957 or 1958 certain of the Emirs as well as the Sardauna of Sokoto himself were beginning to see the Army as more than a pawn in the struggle for power. They were in fact responding to the gradual emergence of a predominance of young Ibo officers in the more senior ranks. Practical counter measures took the form first of an endeavour to persuade scions of ruling houses to seek to obtain commissions in the Army. This informal campaign had little success against the entrenched belief that, while military service might be suitable for the peasants, it was inappropriate for the ruling class. The historic tradition of slave armies in the area was a factor in sustaining this resistance. The only notable recruit at this stage was Hassan Katsina, a younger son of the Emir of Katsina, who has since the coup emerged in a dominant role in Northern Nigeria, having narrowly missed the fate of many other Northern officers in January 1966. Hassan's coolness was shown in his confrontation with Major Nzeogwu on the morning of the coup: his charm and ability, especially as a polo player, helped him to make a success of his career at Sandhurst. Like

Emeka Ojukwu, even as a young officer, because of his connections he always appeared to be of more importance than his rank justified: there seemed to be an awareness of a destiny to uphold the traditions of the North under the guise of a modern progressive outlook. Other attempts by Northern personalities to offset the growing advantage of the Ibos in securing key posts had a quality about them of almost frantic persistence. The establishment of the Nigerian Military School at Zaria led to a drive for recruits from among the adolescents, carried to absurdity in the compound of one Emir who ordered all those males who were in the relevant age group to enlist regardless of their physical condition!

The concern of the Northern leaders for the growing imbalance between the tribes in the officer corps persisted after independence. It led directly in 1962 to the adoption of a quota system for officer recruitment such as already prevailed for other ranks. This was virtually to put into effect a double standard educationally for African officers – a device which had been openly and urgently advocated in Kaduna immediately after independence. At that stage it was even fashionable to blame Lord Lugard for not having imposed Western education on Northern Nigeria and to suggest that there was an expatriate duty to remedy his error by letting African cadets from the region proceed to Sandhurst with a lower level of education than that normally prescribed. Special educational courses during pretraining were also mentioned and there is no doubt that every reasonable effort was made particularly by expatriates to allay these fears and satisfy aspirations. The effect of the new quota system was, of course, to distort the procedure for competitive selection which consisted of a written examination followed by leadership and personality tests and interviews. On the first occasion when the new scheme was operated the Northern quota had to be drawn from a group of entrants which on a strictly competitive basis would have been excluded from selection.

There is no doubt that by 1961–2 the Nigerian Army was coming to be seen as an important factor in the federal power struggle. It was not only the question of the composition of the officer corps which concerned the political leaders: they were thinking in terms of the control and influence which could be exerted over the whole development of the defence forces. The interaction between the political leadership in Kaduna and that in Lagos had ensured that the Ministry of Defence remained in appropriate ministerial hands and that at this stage an expatriate officer was in command of the Army, a feature which the Sardauna of Sokoto saw as essential in preventing the emergence of a senior African commander not likely to be under his influence. The intimate relationships which appeared to exist between officers like Aguiyi-Ironsi and Ojukwu on the one hand and the political leadership of the Ibos on the other were noted. Observers reported the anger caused in Kaduna by the visits paid by the young Captain Ojukwu to Dr Azikiwe when as Governor-General he first stayed in the Northern Capital. There is no denying the atmosphere of conspiracy and counter conspiracy, however notional, which was generated by these essentially tribal fears.

The largely undocumented struggle over the development of an air force was a reflection of the tensions which existed. Late in 1961, a British mission was invited to make recommendations on the establishment of such a force in conjunction with the reconstitution of officer training for the army: a defence academy would provide basic training for officers of all three services. Lengthy negotiations and the provisional appointment of a British Commander for the defence academy followed, but in the end the arrangement broke down. West Germans and Indians at one stage filled the relevant rôles. The source of aid for training, however, is in this context not of particular significance. More important was the fact that a main bone of contention within Nigeria was the choice of an appropriate site for the Air Force training school in which, clearly, technical considerations concerning weather and flying conditions were of first importance. In some quarters, however, the political arguments for siting such an installation near to Kaduna were strong and, because perhaps there were not great technical disadvantages, prevailed. The determination of the Northern political leadership to keep under surveillance important developments which could affect the power structure was undoubtedly a factor in this: their desire to feel that the whole paraphernalia of the Nigerian State was capable of appropriate manipulation was dominant and boomeranged on them in January 1966.

It is undoubtedly possible to exaggerate the extent to which the fission of Nigeria was the result of a struggle between two main power groups for the control of the federation after independence, and it may be that the facts and the impressions formed at this period are capable of another interpretation. A feature of Nigerian society in the weeks and months following independence was, however, the open discussion of the nature of power and means of changing its holders. According to the writer's personal observation all walks of reasonably educated society in Nigeria were sensitive to this problem. Young doctors and civil servants, as well as army officers, and even minor officials seemed alert to possibilities for change which they could not define. The student interest in military training seemed symptomatic of a general agitation. Certainly men from all three regions were affected, though the standpoint of those from the Western region was in a way apart from that of the Fulani aristocracy and the Ibos. Nevertheless, without exception, Yoruba Army officers, from the most senior to the most junior, in all no more than 12 or 13 per cent. of the strength of the officer corps, talked fairly openly of the change which would come when 'a strong man would arise in the East or the West' and the repository of political power would be shifted with the help of the Army.

Political leaders in the Western Region such as Chief Awolowo took a somewhat different and perhaps more realistic stand-point which reflected an appreciation of the relative power-lessness of the Yorubas in such a context: Chief Awolowo's efforts, in particular, were directed at restraining the growth of the armed forces and preventing the development of what he saw as a Latin American type situation. In his autobiography[1] he cited the Trujillo dictatorship in the Dominican Republic as an example of what would not do for Nigeria. His restrained comments, however, were not typical of Nigeria at the begin-ning of 1961 when the wide incidence of hot conspiratorial words might well have encouraged a prediction of an early attempt at a military coup. It is, however, easy to forget two important factors. In the first place, in the African ex-colonial context perhaps more than others, words were often far from deeds and, secondly, there were for some years substantial numbers of expatriates serving in key positions in the Nigerian forces. In practice their mere presence seems to have proved to be an inhibition on politically subversive action.

It is in the context of the climate of opinion about military affairs, a description of which has been attempted above, that the sequence of events which resulted in the coup of January 1966 and the reactions to it have to be considered. The neces-sary facts about the pre-coup Army, Navy, and Air Force are few and fairly straightforward. At the beginning of 1966 there were about ten thousand Nigerians professionally under arms, of whom about eight thousand were in the Army. The Army was organized in normal circumstances into two brigades with headquarters at Apapa, Lagos, and at Kaduna respectively. There were five infantry battalions each of between seven and eight hundred men, three of which were stationed at Abeokuta, Enugu, and Ikeja (near the Lagos international airport) and two more at Kaduna. Detachments from the nearest battalions were located at Ibadan, Lagos, and Kano. Battalions were

[1] Chief Obafemi Awolowo, *Awo* (London, Cambridge University Press, 1960), p. 307.

normally rotated from station to station and battalion headquarters were on occasion located with the outlying detachments. A reconnaissance squadron of light armoured cars was
by its nature fairly mobile: it had been stationed at Kaduna
and operated on the Cameroon frontier, but at the time of the
coup, because of the disturbed political situation in the Western
Region, was actually at Abeokuta. Each battalion centre had
detachments of service units including hospitals, transport,
engineers, and signals. Largely because of the attitude of the
Northern Region Government the greatest concentration of
troops was at Kaduna, where the battalion barracks were con-
veniently close to the Government buildings and Ministerial
residences. The Kaduna district also included the Military
Academy, the Air Force training centre and the ordnance
factory. The Nigerian Military School and the infantry Regimental Depôt were fifty miles away at Zaria. Like most
African armies, the Nigerian at the time of the coup consisted
essentially of Second World War infantry battalions plus certain ancillaries. Virtually all the equipment was of British
origin.

The Nigerian Army had served with relative distinction in
the U.N. force in the Congo and in 1964 replaced the Royal
Marine Commando in helping the Tanzanian Government
through the difficult period after the Army mutiny there. As
far as training and procedure were concerned the Nigerian
force conformed to the Commonwealth pattern which had
proved useful in terms of standardization in the Congo operation. Most Nigerian officers had originally been trained in
Britain though a few had passed through military academies
in other countries. Many had been through preliminary training
in Ghana. Staff and senior officer training was also generally in
British institutions, but one or two officers including Brigadier
Maimalari, the senior Northerner, had been to the Pakistan
Staff College. For two years before the coup the Nigerian
military academy had been under the direction of an Indian

officer: the air force had West German instructors, but the Navy had both British and Indian officers in executive positions. In the Army command positions had been completely Africanized and British officers remained only in a training and advisory capacity.

The process of selecting Nigerian officers began in 1948 under the auspices of Headquarters, West Africa Command: selection was rigorous and young aspirants were required to survive a series of tests and interviews including a final session with the G.O.C. Between 1948 and 1952 men like Ironsi, Ademulegun, and Bassey, who had had proved experience in the ranks, were sent to Britain for short courses at Eaton Hall or Mons Officer Cadet School. In 1952 the first two Nigerians went to Sandhurst: as it happens they were both Northerners, one of whom left the service and the other became Brigadier Maimalari after service as U.N. Liaison officer in the Congo and in other capacities. These recruits from the Northern Region were unfortunately untypical. Such of their compatriots who competed for training places were generally outshone by Ibo rivals who had had superior educational opportunities.

In the Eastern Region secondary education, under both government and mission auspices, was so far developed that the limited employment opportunities did not very readily absorb all the qualified young men to benefit from it. Nor was there any social or political basis in the Eastern Region for a disinclination to join the Army. The result was that by January 1961, three months after independence, sixty out of eight-one Nigerian officers were Ibos, ten Yorubas, and the remaining eleven from the North. The introduction of the quota system, allowing 50 per cent. from the North, in 1962 helped fairly rapidly to redress the strict numerical balance, but the withdrawal of the British had already given many Ibos the opportunity to reach the rank of major and above. Moreover, many of the recent Northern quota at the time of the coup had been Tiv from the Middle Belt, thus reflecting a feature of the other rank composition of the Nigerian Army in modern times. It was nevertheless true that the Army was widely regarded as the least tribalistic of Nigerian institutions even by those who in 1966 appeared by their actions to contradict the validity of this view. In retrospect the refusal to publish tribal statistics of military personnel may seem confirmed as wise: if, on the other hand, they were not compiled for confidential information this was an ostrich-like device. Nevertheless it is true that at the time of the initial coup the three most senior officers promoted to their ranks on a combination of merit and length of service represented respectively the three main regions and that both the battalion commander at Enugu and the Brigadier in Kaduna were Yorubas, while the District Commander in the south was a Kanuri from the north. The cynical, however, would claim that this kind of common-sense dispersion was in itself a precaution against tribalism not far beneath the surface. During an earlier emergency in the Western Region capital, the expatriate G.O.C. had himself had virtually to take command to obviate tribal difficulties in spite of his own delicate position.

The Nigerian military coup of 15 January 1966 did not, of course, derive solely from tensions within the Army itself. Discontent with the distribution of power was more widely based than a single institution but inevitably found its expression in the Army. There was also resentment against corruption in high places both at the federal and regional levels and in the Western Region acute dissatisfaction with the results of the rigged election of October 1965 and the manner of their achievement. Hostility to individual politicians varied in intensity: the Federal Prime Minister, Sir Abubakar Tafawa Balewa, seemed simply to lack the power to pursue his own policies and to control the stupidities of his colleagues: to the Federal Finance Minister, Chief Festus Okotie-Eboh, was popularly and probably rightly attributed massive misapplication of the nation's financial resources, and the Sardauna of Sokoto and Chief S. L. Akintola, Premier of the Western Region, were regarded as having secured to themselves political power and influence beyond that which they could rightly claim to be based on popular support. Suspicion that the Sardauna intended by some means to tighten the Northern grip on the Federal power machine was an important factor in the timing of the coup. Though it will be difficult in view of the deaths of so many of the participants even to establish finally the whole truth, there is no doubt that, by a number of officers who were responsible for the events of 15 January 1966, their action was seen as preëmpting decisive intervention by the opposing faction. If they had not acted then it would have been too late to do so. Since independence the Army had only been required to play a minimal rôle in internal security, notably in the Tiv emergency in the Western Region in 1962. The regional election of 1965 was, however, followed by such a degree of popular disorder that the possibility of using the Army on a large scale had clearly been in the minds of some political leaders. A massive action against opposition elements in the Western Region was not acceptable to Ibo elements at least in the Army and the fear of such a decision seems to have been the key factor in bringing plans for a coup to a degree of ripeness.

Though there are good and obvious grounds for believing that the plotters felt it necessary in any case to wait for the end of the Commonwealth Prime Ministers' conference in Lagos before taking action, the spark which caused the explosion appears to have been a meeting in Kaduna on Friday, 14 January 1966, at which plans were made for military action aimed at settling the state of disorder in the Western Region. No rival incident of sufficient significance to account for the timing of the coup has been reported and there is at least circumstantial evidence from the way in which the operation was conducted to suggest this meeting as its immediate inspiration. In other words, the coup was about the distribution of power in Nigeria which appeared to be about to shift farther to the disadvantage of the opposition groups.

The meeting in Kaduna was probably attended by the Sardauna, the Premier of the Western Region, and senior army officers who must have included Brigadier Sam Ademulegun. Ademulegun, himself a Yoruba, was the likely commander of a strike in the Western Region, but it is legitimate at least to speculate where his real sympathies lay: certainly in time past he had been in close contact with members of the Action Group and his association with Alayande, the headmaster of Ibadan Grammar School, who was Chaplain to the Action Group, was perhaps more than that of an 'alumnus' of the school who had sent his son to follow in father's footsteps. If his loyalty to the ruling establishment was only technical then it was to cost him dear.

It is not known on whose instigation the meeting in Kaduna took place: it is probable that as soon as it finished an officer, probably Lieutenant-Colonel A. Largema, a Northerner from Katsina district who had been trained at Sandhurst, was dispatched to discuss the matter with Major-General Ironsi, the G.O.C. in Lagos. What is more questionable is the extent of the awareness of the Federal Prime Minister that drastic measures were being planned. If he was not privy to the operational discussions which took place then the fears of the dissident army officers that federal power was really northern power and about to be consolidated acquire more substance. The fact that during Friday, 14 January the Government was itself engaged in a minor cabinet reorganization consequent upon the resignation of Dr Jaja Wachuku and his replacement by Mr Mathew Mbu is some evidence that its attention was focused elsewhere than on military moves in the Western Region. The holding of a full-scale but informal military reception that night in Lagos at which General Ironsi was host has also been taken to indicate that the Kaduna meeting, if known of, held no particular significance. The view that a subordinate com-

mander was unlikely to become involved without the knowledge of his ultimate superior, in discussions which might lead
ultimately to the deployment of military forces is not necessarily valid for the then prevailing circumstances in Nigeria
nor indeed in any developing country with a still embryonic
professional tradition. The necessary interchange of information may be hampered not only by inefficient communications
but by delicate personal relationships and conflicts of loyalty.
The rivalry between Ironsi and Ademulegun for the senior
army post had not at the time been wholly forgotten.

The course of events in the early hours of Saturday, 15
January 1966, is now in general fairly clear, though there are
inevitably still areas of uncertainty. Around 3.30 a.m. bodies
of troops under the command of majors and captains began to
take action. The first casualty seems to have been the Northern
colonel with the brief from the Kaduna meeting, which he
could not have had time to convey to Ironsi. He was killed in a
hotel in Ikoyi at about the same time as Sir Abubakar and
Chief Okotie-Eboh were taken from their houses. In the hours
following the communications centres and the Parliament
building were cordoned off and road blocks established on the
main roads. A number of senior Northern officers and one or
two Yorubas were killed in Lagos, notably Brigadier Z.
Maimalari, Colonel K. Muhammed and Lieutenant-Colonel
J. Y. Pam, all of whom had held important command and staff
appointments. The position of Major-General Ironsi during
the early hours of the coup has not been satisfactorily clarified:
some reports suggested that he had been detained for a time
or successfully talked himself out of arrest by mutineers. The
fact is that between the early morning when the end of
'gangsterism and disorder, corruption and despotism' was announced over the radio and 2.30 p.m. in the afternoon when
broadcast reference was made to an 'ill-advised mutiny' and the
work of a 'dissident section of the army' some action must
have been taken in Lagos to restore loyalist control within the

F

force. Though nothing was finally resolved, on the Saturday preliminary discussions involving political and military leaders took place at police headquarters and the path was open to the establishment of a loyalist military régime pledged to restore national unity.

In Kaduna, however, the action of the rebels was not only as violent as in Lagos but more sustained. There at 2.00 a.m. Major Chukwuma Nzeogwu, an Ibo, had contrived an attack on the Northern Premier's house and killed the Sardauna, his wife, and some of his guard. The Northern Regional Governor, Sir Kashim Ibrahim, was arrested and Brigadier Ademulegun and his wife killed in their beds. Major Nzeogwu who emerged as the architect of the whole coup declared martial law 'in the name of the Supreme Council of the Revolution of the Nigerian Armed Forces'. He suspended the Constitution, dissolved the Government and banned all gatherings, except for religious worship: the death sentence was announced as applicable to a wide range of offences and proceedings were started against a number of Northern Ministers. Nzeogwu was undoubtedly a militant Ibo nationalist, but with a commitment to a united Nigeria. Though still a young man when killed in command of a Biafran formation after Biafra's secession from Nigeria, he left behind him a consistent impression of ruthlessness and ambition. He was in the same company at Sandhurst as the Ghanaian coup leader Brigadier A. A. Afrifa but had none of the latter's geniality and tolerance. Within a year or so of his return to Nigeria from Britain, Nzeogwu was at the centre of aggressive incidents in battalion officers' messes and openly hostile to expatriates. Some would say that his open arrogance in his brief hour of victory in Kaduna was his own undoing thereafter his fellow Ibos, Ironsi, and Ojukwu, were reluctant to trust him even though he was in some ways useful as 'the hero of the revolution' in attracting popular support.

Events in Kaduna and Lagos were repeated on a smaller scale in Ibadan where the Regional Prime Minister was killed

but throughout the country after the first few hours the initiative of the mutinous officers, who were small in number,
seems to have drained away. Only fourteen of the coup leaders
have ever been accurately identified and of these all but one or
two were Ibos. Though the leaders proclaimed themselves as
opposed to tribalism and the champions of a united Nigeria,
the facts inevitably put a tribal interpretation on the event in
the eyes of the majority. It is now scarcely worth arguing the
truth of this matter and it may be better that history should
accept the superficial interpretation of the facts and thus
avoid a degree of hypocrisy about the nature of the coup.
Whatever the intentions of the predominantly Ibo mutineers
they succeeded in killing only Northern and Yoruba political
and military leaders – with one exception, namely, Colonel
Arthur Unegbe, who seems to have died doing his apparent
duty as an impartial professional soldier. What is more,
several of those who died, of whom Sir Abubakar and Brigadier
Ademulegun may be taken as the prime examples, were
generally highly regarded and not necessarily totally identified
with narrow political factions. Unlike other coups which have
taken place in Africa there were the signs in this case of certain
of the rebel leaders appearing to enjoy violence and the
destruction of their opponents for its own sake. In Nigeria the
tendency for violence to breed violence was in any case
particularly marked, and on this occasion clearly borne out.

On Sunday, 16 January, those members of the Nigerian
Cabinet who were still available in Lagos met under the chairmanship of Alhaji Zanna Dipcharima and agreed to hand over
the Government temporarily to the Army and the police. At
11.50 p.m. that night the acting President – President Azikiwe
being absent on leave in Britain for health reasons – announced
in a broadcast that the Council of Ministers had unanimously
agreed to hand over the government of the Federation to the
armed forces with Major-General Ironsi as Supreme Commander of the Military Government who promptly decreed

the creation of regional military governments responsible to the Federal Military Government. The basis of the arrangement was that all public services should function as before except that local police forces in the North and West should now be directly subordinate to the Federal Inspector-General of Police. The maintenance of existing external commitments and the continuance of foreign policy were specifically mentioned in Ironsi's statement, which concluded with an appeal to all citizens to co-operate in the maintenance of law and order.

The midnight appeal by the General was followed the following day, 17 January, by the surrender of Major Nzeogwu who declared his loyalty to the General. Nzeogwu's agreement with Ironsi leading to the submission of his sword involved a guarantee of safety and relief from legal proceedings for himself and his supporters and an assurance that the old régime would not be allowed to return to office. The Major claimed that the coup in the North had been organized by only five men, who had not told their units of the purpose of the operation until it was actually in train. He claimed to have commanded the support of the Northerners involved who, he said, were a majority of his force. 'It was truly a Nigerian gathering, and only in the army do you get true Nigerianism.'[1]

The behaviour of Nzeogwu and his 'Supreme Council of the Revolution' in the North was clearly vital to stability and when the appointment of the four military governors was announced on Tuesday, 18 January, the personal relationship between him and Major Hassan Katsina, the designated governor of the North, was itself vital. At this point, Major Nzeogwu, who had clearly hesitated to press forward with his plans at some stage when he saw the tide was beginning to run against his total success, appeared in support of Hassan Katsina and described how Hassan had declared himself on the side of the rebels. In all regions of Nigeria the first reactions, after the recovery

[1] As reported in *West Africa* for 29 January 1966, p. 127.

from initial shock, seem to have been not unfavourable to the new régime. In the North, Hassan Katsina prescribed a programme of reform and economy for the native authorities. In the West disorders were quickly suppressed and Ibadan began to return to normal, and the bans on particular newspapers in the different regions were lifted. Support for the administration was declared by the main political parties, by youth organizations, trades unions, and students. As the military governors assembled for a conference in Lagos, Major Nzeogwu was brought from Kaduna to the capital under the escort of a fellow Ibo, Lieutenant-Colonel Conrad Nwawo, with a guarantee of safe custody.

Having ridden out the storms which might have upset it in its early days the Supreme Military Council set about the restoration of confidence, beginning with three days' official mourning for Sir Abubakar, whose body had been found near Milestone 27 on the Lagos–Abeokuta road. The Military Government was careful to state its intention of honouring all treaty obligations and financial agreements and, in particular, to encourage foreign business enterprise. A clear undertaking was given that no further nationalization of industry was planned and that, in any case, if such a decision had to be taken, adequate compensation would be given. The new administration was thus clearly committed to the continuance of the basic policies previously pursued by Nigeria while at the same time seeking to unify the country and probe the excesses which had led to corruption and a deterioration in confidence.

In spite of a careful beginning, however, relationships between the various groups in the Army and the Government deteriorated almost from the start of the Ironsi administration. In spite or perhaps because of the carefully impartial selection of regional governors to suit local needs, the suspicions and mistrust generated earlier and brought to a head by the events of 15 January inevitably festered. In order to understand the subsequent mutinies by Hausa soldiers and the massacres of

Ibos which followed some further knowledge of the motivation and character of the leading personalities is required.

It is not unreasonable to begin by looking more closely at the position and record of Major-General Johnson Aguiyi-Ironsi who was now head of state. His accession to political power was widely greeted in the British Press in particular: Ironsi was treated as the reluctant hero who would bring all the best qualities of the professional soldier to bear on his new responsibilities, particularly a high degree of political impartiality and a belief that the Army should be itself detached. Expatriate officers who had served with Ironsi in the Nigerian Army found many of the claims hard to accept. Many felt that his efficiency and his incorruptibility were greatly exaggerated, but, more important, they recalled such evidence as there was of his connections with Eastern Region politicians and the attitude which he had tended to adopt on military matters which had implications for the interregional balance of power. It was he, as much as any other officer, who had been vocally in favour of recruitment on educational merit without regard to regional quotas. He had advocated this in the interests of one Nigeria, but had surely not been unaware of the implications for the composition of the Army in tribal terms. He had, in short, in an unsophisticated way, used precisely the arguments about Nigerianism to which Nzeogwu had rhetorically referred. Moreover, many Northerners must have been aware of the mistrust and contempt which the Northern premier had openly displayed towards him. For Ironsi's short tour as Military Liaison Officer in London had been widely thought of as a stalling move arising from the Sardauna's pressure upon the Federal Prime Minister to spoil Ironsi's chances of succeeding Major-General Welby-Everard as G.O.C.

Even if Ironsi had been converted entirely from a politically aware regimental officer into a professional general of detachment in the course of a short three or four years – and this must clearly be admitted to be possible – there were plenty of young officers around him applying pressures of a particular kind. The conditions of Nigeria were and are such that intimacy and confidence is unlikely between men of the different main tribal groups. If Ironsi wanted political advice he was more likely to turn to men like Ojukwu than Katsina, and in any case Ojukwu was much the most intelligent of those soldiers who came to power in January 1966. It was possible for the rarities such as Yakubu Gowon to maintain the trust and friendship, up to a point, of men from different origins. But Gowon from a minority tribe and with his obvious, almost over-honest professionalism was near to being unique. The future of Nigeria after the establishment of the Military Government was then bound to turn on personal relationships as well as on preconceptions about the best line of development for the country. The degree of professionalism which prevailed among the military leadership, the police, and the civil service gave the best chance possible of salvaging the Federal State. Men in key positions at least talked of national unity, but in the event their training and background were not enough to prevent disintegration: the divisive forces operating seemed too great for them to be effectively controlled.

In the first few weeks after the coup the Ironsi régime properly devoted its energies to the consideration of priorities. The small proportion of military in the administration meant a heavy reliance for guidance upon the permanent secretaries of ministries. When the heads of Nigerian overseas missions were recalled to Lagos for discussions at the end of February it was made clear to them, by visits to the Kainji Dam and the Port Harcourt oil refinery, that economic development and commercial activity must be given a high priority. At the same time intensive administrative reforms were being carried out especially of the statutory corporations in which civil servants or technical experts were given control. Like other military administrations, the regional governments in Nigeria displayed what some would regard as puritanical tendencies, reminiscent of 'the rule of the Major-Generals' in England. The governor of the Mid-West region, Lieutenant-Colonel David Ejoor, for instance, made an issue of the unpunctuality of civil servants by closing the doors of ministries at the opening hour of 8 a.m. and shaming the latecomers, of whatever rank, by making them queue outside and haranguing them in public. The overt intention to secure efficiency and to probe corruption was not unpopular with the masses and conformed to the image of the simple, dedicated military officer whose patriotism was unquestioned.

From the first also Ironsi and his advisers prepared for a return to civilian rule by setting up study groups to consider a new constitution without commitment to a particular form. Nevertheless Ironsi's personal preference, no doubt shared by his advisers, for a unitary state was apparent from all the pronouncements and actions of the régime. There were also indications that a presidential system on American lines would be more acceptable in that it would enable the selection of ministerial talent from all walks of public life and make practicable its really efficient deployment in the national interest. The initial plan, however, was to leave the constitutional suggestions to the study groups and to allow the final decision to rest with a constituent assembly. Two factors were, however, important from the start. The first was the inherent preference of those trained on military lines for simple, apparently uncomplicated systems based on merit and with a clear cut hierarchy and allocation and gradation of responsibilities: the second was the inherent difference of attitude between the main regions about the form of state which would best protect their interests.

The activities of the Federal and Regional Governments in the early stages, however, did have the appearance of impartiality. In the Eastern Region the drive against corruption and misuse of public money was particularly severe. Contracts connected with the University of Nigeria, Nsukka, were re-

voked and the activities of, for instance, the former regional
Minister of Town Planning, who was charged with 'corruptly
accepting' £7,500 and a Volkswagen car were closely investi-
gated. There was some difficulty in effectively prohibiting the
holding of political meetings, but this was overcome by greater
vigilance on the part of the authorities. On 5 March 1966 Dr
Michael Okpara, former premier of the Eastern Region and
leader of the National Council of Nigerian Citizens (N.C.N.C.)
and nine other politicians were placed in detention 'in the
interest of the security of Nigeria'. In the North Lieutenant-
Colonel Hassan as Military Governor made at least a token
resistance to exclusiveness in appointing the regional civil
service: in a Press interview on 14 March he claimed that he
did not recognize the former government's policy of 'northern-
ization' and said that anyone from any part of Nigeria could
get a job in the North. At this stage the supreme military
council seemed to have devoted time to such matters as the
development of a uniform educational system for Nigeria.

Towards the end of March General Ironsi elaborated at its
opening session in far greater detail than before the tasks in
front of the Constitutional Review Study Group on which
progress towards a return to civilian rule clearly depended.
He urged them to 'identify constitutional problems' in the
'context of One Nigeria'. He said that 'in the new order of
things, there should be no place for regionalism and tribal conscience, subjugation of public service to personal aggrandise-
ment, nepotism and corruption'. It was, he claimed, 'apparent
to all Nigerians that rigid adherence to regionalism had been
the bane of the last régime and one of the main factors which
contributed to its downfall'. The Group's terms of reference are
important in reflecting both the basic premises and the determined impartiality of the review being undertaken:

'To identify those faults in the former Constitution of
Nigeria which militated against national unity and against

the emergence of a strong Central Government; to ascertain how far the powers of the former Regional Governments fostered regionalism and weakened the Central Government; to consider the merits and demerits of (a) a Unitary form of Government, (b) a Federal form of Government, as a system of Government best suited to the demands of a developing country like Nigeria . . . without hampering the emergence of a strong, united, democratic Nigeria. The Group is to suggest possible territorial divisions of the country; to examine voting system, electoral act and revision of voters' register. It is to consider the merits and demerits of (1) One-Party System, (2) Multi-Party System, as a system best suited to Nigeria, and the extent to which party politics fostered tribal consciousness, nepotism and abuse of office; to determine the extent to which professional politics contributed to the deficiencies of the past regime, and the extent to which regionalism and party politics tended to violate traditional chieftaincies and institutions and to suggest possible safeguards.'

In the circumstances it might be argued that it would have been better for the dominant elements in the Military Government to declare themselves at an early stage fully committed to the idea of a unitary state and so short circuit the discussions. If this could have led to immediate consideration of the most convenient administrative structure to replace the unwieldy regions then an early deterioration into interregional rivalries might perhaps have been avoided.

Though in many ways the signs were ominous the achievements of the Ironsi régime over the first three months of its existence were considerable and clearly reflected the attractive features of military administration. In the first place Nigeria began briefly to enjoy a period largely free of violent disorders. There had been the disturbances in the Delta area led by Isaac Boro and there was continued banditry in the North and West but the small army backed by the police force seemed to have established the writ of the régime throughout the large country and this had been achieved with a far greater degree of tolerance of newspaper criticism and political discussion than is normally associated with army rule. The apparent consent of the people seemed to stem from the satisfaction felt with the ending of the regional system with its opportunities for the exploitation of power and corruption. The continuous references to 'One Nigeria' appeared to have checked the fission which had set in before the Army disorder. The question of the future form of government for Nigeria was now open to discussion.

Nevertheless the traumatic effect of the murders on 15 January had not worn off: in fact, the relative lack of reaction in the North at the time of the news of the deaths of the Sardauna and Sir Abubakar may not have helped the release of tension. Clearly regional and tribal feeling could not be eliminated by a stroke of a pen or a few speeches: the sincerity of the principal personalities in this respect perhaps ought not to be questioned for there is not public evidence for doing so, but it is not difficult to imagine the continued fostering of suspicion behind the scenes which is typical of petty public figures in the intervals between crises. Whatever the truth of the matter it was scarcely possible to obliterate the belief that the Army's intervention in politics was only an assertion of Ibo aspirations. Everything, therefore, depended on the ability of the supreme military council to handle the affairs of the Northern Region with such delicacy that the conviction of its good intentions should be firmly established. The choice and rôle of Colonel Hassan Katsina was of great importance and in this respect it would be wrong to dismiss as sentimental the military camaraderies of officers trained in the same tradition.

More recently the personal relationship of Gowon and Ojukwu, 'Jack' and 'Emeka', sustained by long telephone calls, was a factor in postponing the final breakdown between Nigeria and Biafra, and there is no reason to suppose that on a more casual level this tie did not keep the Supreme Commander and the Military Governors from open and angry dissension. Indeed there is some evidence occasionally detectable in conversation that in the regions there were some who were critical of their leaders because of the danger that professional friendships would impair the ability of the governors to protect local interests.

The Civil Services of Nigeria in general seem to have felt a sense of liberation under the new auspices: senior civil servants in the North did not, it is true, look with favour upon plans to unify the services, but the military administration gave them a fresh opportunity to serve the people free of undue sectional or corrupt influences. The ability of the military to set themselves up as arbiters or referees in such situations and to provide a clear framework for action is an important feature of their political rôle of which there are numerous examples in recent history. It is when they have to go beyond this point, cease to try to neutralize the political forces and attempt to devise policies that the difficulties arise, as the situation in Sierra Leone in 1967 and 1968 has perhaps revealed most clearly. Indeed it can be argued that in many cases military government involves a political moratorium after which evolution continues in the same or possibly a different direction from that before the coup.

The essential problems of the Nigerian Military Government were two and closely related. In some way they had to achieve a working degree of national unity and to provide scope for a basically sound economy and economic policy to work. In a sense the corruption and incompetence which had hindered the latter, in spite of a large improvement in the balance of payments in 1965, was a product of regionalism and tribalism. The military régime not only had increasing oil production and developing secondary industry, but a generous attitude on the part of the World Bank on which to rely. On the whole, international organizations as well as individual Western states have responded well to appeals for financial support from countries where moderate military régimes have come to power. But the capacity of such a régime to tackle internal economic problems is limited. It was estimated that the Nigerian administration could save at once £26 m. a year by dismantling the apparatus of regional government but it was hampered by its very nature in any attempt to provide employment to stimulate the economy or, for instance, to control rents. Austerity is almost inevitably a feature of the circumstances in which military régimes must operate and this does not allow for the satisfaction of the vocal wage-earners on whose consent in the end the Government will rest.

Thus as a policy-making body the Nigerian Military Government of Ironsi was no stronger than might have been expected. Its superficial achievement was an unusual stability due as much to a choice of personalities and the ability of the Supreme Commander to control the young men who had engineered the coup in the first instance as to anything else. The General, however, had not only to contend with the national problems but with the impatience of these young officers if progress was not made in ways that they thought it should be. There was always the possibility of military intergenerational conflict especially in view of the way in which Nzeogwu's initiative had been diverted into establishment channels. There was within months of the coup talk of a Nasser emerging to supersede Ironsi's Neguib, and the name most frequently mentioned was that of Ojukwu, but there was no proven substance to such a move nor any time for it to develop.

Whether there were any conspiratorial developments within the Army is difficult to assess, but the absorption of the military governors in regional affairs seemed total. Colonel Ojukwu emerged as an outspoken critic of tribalism. In May he decreed that all references to tribes in government documents in Eastern Nigeria should be expunged. Public servants of all categories must be judged without regard for their places of origin. It was his view that Nigerians must be allowed to live and work freely anywhere in the whole country. At an earlier stage he had criticized advertisements for government scholarships which required applicants to be children of parents of Eastern Region origin. He opened the competition to all children resident in the particular area concerned regardless of tribe. This was in line with Ibo opposition to the regional and provincial quota systems for army recruitment which had generally been regarded by Northern officers as hypocritical as far as the national interest went and guaranteed to strengthen the Ibo position – in other words, in the new situation only a harmless gesture to attract international political credit.

During May 1966 after four months in office the Nigerian Military Government set a three-year limit on its tenure of office – a period which left some people doubting whether the officers' reluctance to govern was genuine. The fact that the announcement was accompanied by a formal ban on all eighty-one listed political parties and on tribal organizations of a political character reinforced the doubts. The continuance of political activity through tribal societies was, however, a factor leading to this decision. Only a firm public stand on the part of the Military Government could show where they stood on this matter and their determination to have real stability before the politicians were allowed to return. At this point, however, it was clear that the régime had to rethink its position and consider how it could adapt itself from being a holding administration into a government capable of developing policy.

What in the new circumstances was to be the rôle of the senior civil servants who had been running the ministries? Were they in effect to become ministers? Much more important and more typical of the inevitable problems of military government was the question of consultation, of determining in some way means of achieving and sustaining a popular consensus. The nature of military management with its strictly hierarchical structure and its precise 'rule of thumb' procedures must entail a growing divorce from public opinion, after the first enthusiasm has worn off, unless special devices are adopted. The fact that the Nigerian Army was small and not well known throughout the country was now a hindrance: unlike the Ghana Army leaders in a much smaller and more homogeneous country, those in Nigeria were not at all well known in popular terms. The Nigerian military stations too, especially the concentration on the outskirts of the Kaduna cantonment, had not been conducive to reducing the normal isolation of armies with their concentrated family and social life actually at the place of work. The banning of political activity at a late stage meant that on the whole it was less likely that Nigeria's leaders would keep in touch with popular opinion. This was not in any case going to be easy now that the Army leaders were emerging as generally committed to a unitary state without any regional grouping of provinces.

The dangers were to some extent offset by the notable freedom of the Press at this stage which was far greater than had prevailed before the coup. The newspapers clearly had an important two-way information function to perform. The continued activity of the trades unions, with perhaps their political aspect now inhibited, was another factor assisting in this process.

General Ironsi's radio broadcast on 23 May 1966, which also dealt with the matters of a renewed national development plan, food prices, university education, and rent control, appeared to set the seal on unitary government and to mark the formal end of the federal structure. There was no reason for this to have been a shock to interested parties in the light of what had gone before, and the content of the broadcast was still capable of being construed as applicable only to the three years of military rule. The Military Governor of the Northern Provinces went out of his way to relate this to military thinking – 'We in the Army have got a unified command and it is the method we are used to.' He subsequently assured a gathering of Emirs and Chiefs that what had now been decided would not necessarily apply permanently to the constitutional arrangements which would operate when civilian rule was restored. Emphasis was laid in other quarters on the limited duration of the ban on political parties and attention drawn to the phrase 'this corrective government' as indicative of the military cast of thought.

A weekend of riots in the North followed the speech and in their motivation lay clues to the more serious disorders which followed in July and September. To some extent they seem to have been inspired by politicians finally disappointed at the considerable postponement of the prospect of their return to power and the perquisites that went with it and at the realization that their previous control over the destiny of Nigeria, arising from the distribution of population, had slipped away. Observers reported the display by demonstrators of placards with slogans such as 'Let there be Secession' and 'No Unitary Government without Referendum' but there was general agreement that these demonstrations did not represent a considered rejection of the constitutional proposals: there was little doubt concerning their tribalistic, essentially anti-Ibo nature. In all more than ninety people were reported killed, most of them in Kano, where the Sabon Gari or 'strangers' quarter' was cordoned off by the Army's second battalion after reports of attacks on the Ibo residents. Objectives for attack included the offices of the Northern Nigerian Marketing Board, the Provincial administration building, and reputedly Roman Catholic churches run by American missionaries. The Military Government made reference to foreign elements inciting to riot, but what they meant by this is not clear.

In a broadcast appeal[1] to the people of Northern Nigeria the Military Governor said that he would not hesitate to declare any disturbed area under martial law. Once again he apologized

[1] See *West Africa*, No. 2557 of 4 June 1966, p. 639.

for the decrees on the unification of the civil services and the abolition of federalism as being interim and temporary measures. He particularly stressed that the arrangement with regard to the civil service was not intended to give advantage to any particular section of the community. 'Some areas are more advanced than others, and it is our intention that the national government will give massive assistance to less developed areas so that they can catch up as soon as possible with the more developed areas.' The whole objective would be to ensure fair representation in the Government. The disturbances in the North showed clearly how tenuous the control by the Military Government in fact was and how widespread the disinclination to trust its intentions to look after all sections of the population impartially.

Subsequent renewal of violence, notably in Katsina, the Military Governor's home town, led him to comment, perhaps unwisely, that the reputation for good behaviour which Northerners had acquired after the events in January was at stake. He continually reiterated the view that no permanent changes in the governmental structure had been nor would be made without consulting the people. He stressed the extent to which the civil service would still be run locally and the plans proposed for crash education and training programmes. The events at the end of May and the views of the traditional leaders in the North brought to bear on the Military Government irresistible pressures to modify its plans. In June, after a two-day meeting, the council agreed to announce that there would be a referendum eventually to approve the reformed structure of the state and sought to reassure the nation 'that this decree was designed to meet the demands of military government under a unified command and to enable it to carry out its day-to-day administration'. Both Federal and Regional Military Governments then made a considerable effort to make clear their intentions, but the flight from the North on the part of Ibos by public and private transport especially from Kaduna had already begun and from this time onwards there were frequent rumours of scares within army units about one tribal group taking violent action against another.

During June and July the efforts of the members of the Military Government showed a continued concern for the basic problems with which the administration was faced; while Lieutenant-Colonel P. A. Anwunah announced a drive for greater efficiency and punctuality in the civil service, a decree was published in Lagos empowering the confiscation of that part of a person's wealth which had been acquired by corruption or abuse of public office and in the Mid West steps were taken against owners of more than one plot of land in government residential areas. This was in line with the notion of 'corrective' government which Ironsi had more than once propounded. More significant, however, was the meeting held in Ibadan at the end of July of twenty-four emirs, chiefs, and natural rulers from different parts of Nigeria. This was addressed by the Supreme Commander himself and demonstrated the thoughtfulness of his advisers with regard to keeping open all means of communication with the population. The vacuum created by the temporary removal of politicians has in several countries of Africa given the traditional rulers a new opportunity to carve a niche for themselves in a modern state. The Military Government was clearly recognizing the value of support from this quarter in political as well as administrative terms, though presumably it had no intention of allowing the chiefs to take over the rôles left vacant by the politicians.

The address to the conference of chiefs was almost General Ironsi's last act, for the following night he, along with Lieutenant-Colonel Fajuyi, the Military Governor of the West, was seized in Ibadan by mutineers and later executed near by. The counter coup, for this it was, was clearly on tribal lines, the objects of attack in each station being the Ibo officers and men. The timing may well have been due to the relative ease with which Ironsi could be isolated while visiting Ibadan: events in each station followed a similar pattern at Abeokuta and Ikeja. On the airport road in Lagos Brigadier Ogundipe made an abortive attempt to regain control of the rebel forces, but it was clear that the main units there, in the West generally, and at Kaduna were in the same state of rebellion. Ogundipe, a Yoruba, refused to assume command and, for almost a day, Nigeria had no government. Only Gowon's willingness apparently to negotiate on behalf of the rebels and his concern for Nigeria enabled a working solution to be found, though already, and perhaps realistically, Lieutenant-Colonel Ojukwu in Enugu was suggesting that 'the brutal and planned annihilation of officers of Eastern Nigerian origin' had cast serious doubt as to whether the people of Nigeria could ever hope to live together sincerely as one nation. At one stage, moreover, the rebels at Ikeja had been reported as demanding the secession of the West and the North. Lieutenant-Colonel Yakubu Gowon thus took over Ironsi's rôle faced with the undoubted fact that the basis for Nigerian unity had been dissolved, which he bravely interpreted as meaning simply that the proposed unitary structure was totally impracticable and that Nigeria would have to be restructured. The prospect of effecting this on the basis of military government weakened by the decimation of the military leadership was never great. The chances of reconstructing what was in any sense a Nigerian Army were slim: the Army itself had failed to end the domination of Nigerian politics by tribalism and had in the process virtually destroyed itself.

The failure of the Ironsi administration to ward off the dangers of a major explosion must be attributed in large measure to the rash nature of the original coup led mainly by Ibo majors. Though Ironsi appeared to attempt persistently to put forward a national rather than a regional or tribal image, his failure firmly to deal with the original mutineers was seen as condonation of the original murders, if not as actual proof of complicity in them. This combined with a programme of re-organization and reform, especially of the civil service, which appeared likely to put Northerners at a competitive disadvantage, aroused and sustained deep suspicion which was no doubt fed from many sources. All the traditional stories of the evil intentions of and appalling atrocities by the other tribe which had long been a feature of Nigerian life were revived and refurbished. This produced an uncontrollable situation, not because of tribalism itself, but because of the realization by majority and minorities alike that control over the sources of power was at stake. Events from the end of July through to October 1966 involving large-scale murder of the Ibo population in a number of centres transformed the situation and unless something like General Ankrah's intervention at Aburi had worked a miracle or some very loose federation could have been quickly agreed on, the outcome of the secession of Biafra and civil war was almost inevitable. Certainly with the reconstruction of the Nigerian forces and preparation for war this ceases to be a valid example for comparative purposes of military intervention in politics and the narrative of Biafra's road to secession requires to be told in other terms.

The tragic Nigerian affair certainly raises questions about the validity of attempting to study military intervention in politics as a separate phenomenon or indeed tribalism as such. The fact of the Army in any state having at its disposal certain equipment, men, arms, and skills gives it power of a kind. The crucial question is the extent to which the officers and men concerned reflect and are identified with the foci of power, economic and political, in the nation as a whole.

In retrospect the original Nigerian military coup of 15 January 1966 had a number of unexplained features. While it is fairly safe to assume that the Premiers of the West and North were prime targets for the rebels, we do not known for certain whether the Federal Prime Minister was killed or the Prime Minister of the East spared by accident. Nor can we be sure whether General Ironsi was innocent or not of implication in the original outbreak. What is clear is that whatever the intentions and whatever the motives, the Ibo faction appeared to emerge on top in spite of the deposition of their politicians who, though alive, were not at the time accorded especially generous treatment. Like most African coups, the Nigerian was partly about corruption and malpractices and a general disgust with wealthy politicians. But more accurately it was about power complicated by the fact that the various factions were distinguishable on a tribal basis. By ability and opportunism and for geographical reasons the Ibos had secured in socio-economic terms a privileged position in Nigeria. They had the wealth, more particularly since the development of the oil resources, and they had the jobs because they had allowed and encouraged the development of Western secondary education on their soil on a large scale. More particularly they had a preponderance of key jobs in the Army, Police, and Civil Service. In other words, they had made much more progress into the modern world than had their Northern neighbours. The one thing they lacked from the first was political power which corresponded in any way with their economic power, and they lacked it because their population was relatively small in relation to that of the whole of Nigeria. An early attempt to ally political power with economic power or to share it broke down: the original government of independent Nigeria had been formed of an alliance of the main parties of the North and East, but it turned out not to be a viable alliance. It was the determination of the conservative Northern majority to retain power which brought into play the only forces in the East which appeared to be capable of breaking that power. A situation which cannot be changed by constitutional means invites the use of violent measures in the same way as a life president can only be removed by force or assassination. On this basis the wild talk of the early sixties about breaking the power of the North and action by the strong Ibo military officer élite was almost inevitable once the attempt to bargain between regional political organizations had failed.

The ejection of the Nigerian army into politics can be attributed to the operation of the forces already mentioned along with the fact that only the N.C.N.C. of Nigerian political parties was committed to a unitary Nigerian government at an early stage: it then allowed itself to be forced back again on to the regional stage so that nationalist politics in Nigeria were locally and tribally based. It may be that the uneven distribution of economic wealth made this to some extent inevitable. The events which brought matters to a head were the publication of the disputed census in 1963 and the rigged election in the Western Region in 1965, which it must be remembered finally thwarted the disintegrated Action Group which like the N.C.N.C. had briefly adopted a Nigerian rather than a regional standpoint. The young Yoruba officers mentioned earlier and the Ibos who effected the coup had in fact much in common and to them may be reasonably attributed a resentment at the growth of regionalism and at the failure of the politicians to go any way towards realizing the greatness of Nigeria. In new states militant nationalism and implicit almost traditional – in professional terms – patriotism are likely to coincide. It is indeed more likely that Major Nzeogwu and his fellows were idealists truly concerned with one free Nigeria than indiscriminate murderers even though their actions and the consequences of them justified the latter title.

The overthrow of the Federal Government and the emergence of General Ironsi as a kind of saviour was popular because it appealed to a wide range of elements in the population, especially in the South. The apparent suppression of tribalism and the shift of power away from the North made it appear that a lasting success had been achieved, but the Military Government in the end failed because it did not sufficiently appreciate the political realities and postponed the creation of a political basis for the administration. But is not such a failure inherently the penalty of military rule? If political parties are banned can the return to a political society be other than chaotic? The mutiny in July 1966, in fact, finally forced the Easterners into a position which they had never generally held before – that of wanting strong regions within a loose federation rather than strong central government based on a conglomeration of small states. The pendulum has swung in Nigeria from regionalism to a unitary state and back in recent years. At each stage in the development of Nigeria, because of the original acceptance by the majority of a regional structure, at any one time one of the main regional groups, the West, the North, or the East has had virtually no say in the government of the country, i.e. no share in formal political power. The situation became critical when the region most strongly represented in the key ranks in the Army was in this position: the coup however, put the North, the region numerically strongest in the Army, into this state and it retaliated. The interaction between the ethnic composition of any army and the distribution of power at the centre has never been more clearly illustrated than in Nigeria.

VII · The Case of Ghana

In some ways it is surprising that the régime of President Nkrumah in Ghana was not overthrown by military action at an earlier stage in its history than 24 February 1966. But to take this view means ignoring some of the important features of the Ghanaian situation. In the first place, Kwame Nkrumah had pioneered the route to freedom from colonial rule in Africa. In so doing he had proclaimed, whether from megalomania or not, an idealism concerning African unity which appealed to the youth of Ghana as well as in other states of the continent. Ghana was, moreover, not only at independence more economically sound but essentially more homogeneous and, therefore, more politically stable than other African states. In other words Ghana was nearer to being one nation than most of her contemporaries and to some extent ripe for exploitation and leadership by a man who sought to glorify Ghanaian and thereby African achievement. As a country also it possessed an exceptionally well developed élite, including an efficient civil service and sound security forces in which a professional code of behaviour was not shallowly rooted. The superior development of Ghanaian society in African terms to a certain extent inhibited the emergence of open protest and dissent against an authoritarian régime: professionalism on the part of public servants sustained the administration's efficiency for a long period in spite of political lunacy and at the same time provided a major deterrent to political action on the part of that élite. Pronouncements by the leaders of the 1966 coup almost invariably stress their original reluctance to be involved in unconstitutional action and on the evidence available there is little reason to doubt the genuineness of these sentiments. The seeds of the Ghana coup inevitably germinated slowly and it is, therefore, necessary to look back at least to 1959 to understand fully its origins and motivation.

In 1957 newly independent Ghana inherited from the British a small army of three battalions of infantry and ancillary troops which was still commanded by British officers. There is reason to believe that at this stage Nkrumah was not altogether dissatisfied with this situation. Africanization of the officer corps was proceeding at a reasonable speed and was already being reinforced by the selection of more senior ranks for staff and specialist training. In the next three years plans were made to accelerate officer production and to expand the Army over a period of years to two full brigades: at the same time embryonic new forces were established – first a navy and then an air force. At this stage the foreign support for the Ghana armed forces came primarily from Britain, though Indians and Israelis were introduced to help the development of the Air Force. Though Nkrumah was already cultivating Communist assistance in other fields, he had not by 1960 apparently tried to invite military aid from that quarter. The key post of Chief of Defence Staff was held by a Briton, Major-General A. G. V. Paley, who handed over to Major-General H. T. Alexander in January 1960. The extent of Nkrumah's reliance on the advice of these officers is in itself an interesting subject and certainly the eventual dismissal of Alexander on 22 September 1961 was an event of considerable political significance.

The forces for which Alexander had assumed responsibility in 1960 were already developing a sense of pride as symbols of the new state. In a small new state the Army is necessarily less isolated from political developments than in advanced Western countries, particularly where there is one all pervasive political party and not much formalized opposition. Nevertheless, as far as could be determined by first-hand inquiry at the time, there were very few military personnel in 1960 who were 'up to their necks in party politics' in spite of the personal promotion advantages which might have been assumed to accrue to individuals who chose this line of action. More common was the expression of similar criticisms of political decisions and activities to those made by senior civil servants, which might be best attributed to a genuine conviction that what was being done was not in the best interests of Ghana or most likely to establish her reputation among the nations of the world. The armed forces, which General Alexander took over, were in the process of adjusting to the implications of the court martial of Major Benjamin Awhaitey and the subsequent Granville Sharp commission of inquiry convened by the Government. Both affairs centred round an alleged conspiracy against Nkrumah supposedly involving an attempt by the opposition M.P., R. R. Amponsah, to involve army personnel in the plot. The inquiry spent much time investigating such matters as arrangements to purchase uniforms from a dealer in London and a gathering, which seemed to consist of officers trained in Britain, at the Seaview Hotel, Accra, which was almost certainly no more than a birthday party. In the event the chairman of the Commission disagreed with its other members as to whether a conspiracy had actually taken place. Nkrumah's main objective in convening it had certainly been to discredit the opposition. Whether he already suspected the possibility of army disloyalty is not clear, but there was no doubt about the effect of the whole episode. The army officer corps reacted by adopting a stance of political neutralism: most of them thereafter declined to make any comments whatsoever on the political situation. Some like the then Major Charles M. Barwah, in particular, had clearly studied the report of the inquiry in detail and were prepared to discuss it almost academically; others accepted its lesson, that there was no future in dabbling in politics. Throughout 1959 and 1960 until well after the Ghana Army had become involved in the U.N.

Congo operation the memories of Awhaitey's fate, whatever the justice of it, dominated the attitudes of the normal Ghanaian officer.

The early months of 1960 were characterized by Nkrumah's taking a more constructive interest in the armed services. Late in 1959 he had not only initiated the training of an air force but he had spent much time discussing, mainly with expatriates, officer provision. The result was the establishment in March 1960 of the Ghana Military Academy at Teshie, east of Accra on the road to Tema; here a cadet course was organized on Sandhurst lines with a British Commandant, Director of Academic Studies, and supporting staff of whom a small minority were initially Ghanaian. The objective was accelerated Africanization on the best terms possible since it was clear that Britain, India, and other countries prepared to offer training places could not meet Ghana's immediate need. Nkrumah's continuance of British aid at this time in so far as it was positively conceived may be interpreted as deriving from a desire to sustain the allegedly apolitical tradition: his sensitivity on this point had been reflected earlier in his cancellation of a training arrangement with Pakistan soon after the military coup there which brought General Ayub Khan to power. At this stage the military advisers closest to him were well aware of a certain ambivalence in his attitude to the question of Africanization even though one view prevailed.

In July 1960 the establishment of the Republic of Ghana with Nkrumah as President was followed closely by the Congo crisis. These two events can in retrospect be seen to have marked the beginning of the real deterioration in Nkrumah's relations with the Army and its attitude towards him. Though for at least a further two years he cultivated the officer corps with banquets and other signs of anxiety to maintain their loyalty, the combination of a greater power of interference by the President in military affairs with the strain of actual operations in the international limelight created foci of inflammation which enlarged over the years as the régime became more fearful and oppressive.

The revision of the Ghana Constitution in 1960 was important in this connection in that it entrenched the position of the President in a number of ways. Effectively only the size and formal initiative of raising armed forces rested with Parliament thereafter. The head of state acquired powers to dismiss or suspend military personnel and to exercise a veto on an officer's authority. He could require the defence forces to engage in an operation for any of a number of specific purposes or for 'any other expedient purpose'. He had the right to call up reserve forces and integrate them into the regular forces. The President's authority was such that in effect he could determine a state of war. The legal provision specifically absolved him from the absolute necessity of following proffered advice and there was apparently no requirement for prior parliamentary approval. He was, as Supreme Commander, 'ex officio' Chairman of the Defence Committee and the Chiefs of Staff Committee. Officers were commissioned in accordance with his constitutional authority and swore allegiance to him. Thus he could not only appoint and prefer individual officers but initiate developments in such a way as to commit sections of the Army to the régime. Above all he could of his own action involve the armed forces in adventures in anticipation of parliamentary approval, which with the declaration of a one party state was not hard to obtain. Those arbitrary actions with regard to the forces which President Nkrumah did subsequently take and the associated fear of what he could and might do very significantly accumulated and contributed over the years between 1960 and 1966 to the encouragement of attitudes within the officer corps which ultimately made the coup possible.

The immediate involvement of the Ghana Army in the Congo in July 1960 was in part made practicable by the President's newly acquired authority, but there is no evidence that any sections of it would have wished to oppose such a decision. The rôle of the Ghanaian, as of the Nigerian, contingent there has been frequently described. It is the effect on the components of that force of the experience there which has now to be considered. Broadly speaking this experience was successful and creditable, and this developed the Ghanaian soldiers pride and confidence in themselves. Whereas previously they were untried, now the wild unpredictability of events in the Congo helped forge them into a professional body. There were risks and temptations, but on the whole these were in the end overcome and the leaders of the national army of the new Ghana began to merge. They inevitably compared their discipline and effectiveness with that of other contingents and they had laudatory reports in the world's press. They had skills in such matters as riot and internal security drills which were superior to those of the white neutral troops of Sweden and Ireland to whom, therefore, they had something to teach. They came to despise the chaotic disorder into which the Congolese people and the 'Force Publique' had got themselves and they began to become distrustful of political leadership, first of all that of others and then their own.

It was not only the special initiative of Nkrumah in providing Ghanaian troops for the Congo in anticipation of U.N. intervention which tended to place those troops in an ambiguous position: it was the special relationship of the President with Patrice Lumumba. The relationship of Ghana's contingent to the U.N. command was continually embarrassed by the activities of the two Ghanaian political representatives in Leopoldville, Andrew Djin and N. A. Welbeck. These two came to symbolize to many of the more intelligent and better educated Ghanaian officers what were described by one young battalion adjutant as 'the clown-like antics of the politicians'. A series of confused, even ludicrous episodes not always creditable to the courage of the political representatives in question began a process which was finally to erase confidence in the political leadership from the minds of many officers. As the service of successive battalions in the Congo was rotated, so each unit returned home expressing in private a consistency of reaction which was surprising and certainly permeated down to junior N.C.O.s. On the whole the Ghanaian Army in the Congo managed a difficult situation of conflicting pressures from the U.N. and its home government with considerable skill, though at one stage a major unit had to be moved from Leopoldville to the provinces in order to reduce the tensions.

In political terms then the Congo operation was a searing and formative experience for the Ghana contingent. Contemporary evidence and impressions tend to support the views ultimately expressed retrospectively by Colonel A. A. Afrifa in his book *The Ghana Coup, 24th February 1966*.[1]

> The fault was that of our politicians at home who had placed us under the command of the United Nations, and at the same time taken active and sinister sides in the whole Congo affair . . . Kwame Nkrumah had placed us in a terrible dilemma through an unbridled political adventure. He appointed and directed a stream of stupid ambassadors like A. Y. K. Djin and N. A. Welbeck . . . Could it be that we had been sent to the Congo to foster the ambition of Kwame Nkrumah?

To this he attributes the murder of Ghanaian soldiers by the Congolese at Port Francqui. Thereafter the fear that the President would commit them to some potentially disgraceful and disastrous adventure was a matter of intense concern to some Ghanaian officers. The experience of service in the Congo lasted nearly three years in all.

A succession of events at home, thereafter, tended to reinforce the developing distrust of politicians. The general strike starting in Western Ghana in 1961 involved the use of army units and the virtual ringing of Accra, the capital, by

[1] London, 1966, p. 66.

force under the command of Brigadier Barwah who appeared
from that time onwards to be especially trusted by Nkrumah.
At that time, with the workers in revolt a coup could easily
have been staged, but there was no such attempt: by this may
be measured the reluctance of army officers to act uncon-
stitutionally and the justice of many of Afrifa's subsequent
remarks on this subject.

The coincidence of the ending of the Sekondi-Takoradi
strike with the dismissal of eighty British officers including
General Alexander on 22 September 1961 reflected both
Nkrumah's largely unwarranted doubts about the willingness
of such officers to carry out his orders in a serious internal
political crisis and his increasing confidence about the provision
of aid by Communist states. General Alexander and the senior
African officers already knew of the tentative arrangement to
send cadets to Russia for training and it was clearly a notion
which they resisted with differing degrees of vigour according
to their personal standing in the situation. General Alexander
has made it clear[1] that the difference of opinion over Nkrumah's
decision to take advantage of Soviet military aid was one
fundamental cause of his dismissal and in a letter[2] to Colonel
(now General) Ankrah who was then serving in the Congo
refers to the attitudes of S. J. A. Otu and N. A. Aferi towards
the move. The expressed fear was that the Army would eventually become divided by officer cliques trained in entirely
different traditions. In the event the threat to send 400 young
men to Russia was never fulfilled: such a total would have represented more than half the adequately educated secondary
school leavers for the year and the cream had already been
skimmed to go to Britain and to the Ghana Military Academy.
Only sixty-eight of poor quality were found to go to Moscow
and, while their individual experiences are not known, it is

[1] Major-General H. T. Alexander, *African Tightrope*, London, 1965,
p. 92.
[2] Alexander, ibid., appendix D, pp. 147–8.

clear that few if any actually completed a full course and they did not represent a significant complication when they eventually returned to Ghana. In the same month as the decision was taken, Canadian officers arrived to help with officer training in Ghana and by May 1962 a British Joint Services Training Team nearly two hundred strong was at work in Ghana. The incident of the cadets for Russia is, therefore, more important for its effect on the attitudes of senior Ghanaian officers than for its practical consequences.

From 1962 onwards the upward spiral of Nkrumah's fears for his own security began to affect the Army and the police forces to a far greater extent than had been the case following the Awhaitey affair. The attempted assassination by bomb at Kulungugu in the north of Ghana on 1 August 1962 followed by an explosion near Flagstaff House, Accra, early in September evidently caused the President totally to rethink the problem of his own protection. He sought help from Communist countries in constructing a personal guard unit and tried to establish tighter personal control over the police force. The fact that he had now been voted President for life clearly placed him in a more exposed position in that there was no longer a remote possibility of removing him by constitutional means. The suspicion that army personnel were implicated in the Kulungugu bomb affair at least through the provision of grenades caused him to turn to non-Africans for protection. At this stage he certainly created the President's Own Guard Regiment (P.O.G.R.) and may have begun to train a separate secret army, the evidence for which is somewhat slender and based on material published by the new régime after the coup. Certainly stocks of Russian weapons were accumulated, but it is not altogether clear whether these were for a new army or to provide for the equipment of foreign 'freedom fighters' who were undoubtedly being trained in Ghana at this time.

The regular army's reaction to these manoeuvres, which were accompanied by a run-down of equipment and general neglect of their interests, was naturally one of resentment. At an earlier stage there had been some attempt to install political agents or 'commissars' in army units which inevitably involved a disruption of the Army hierarchy and the possibility that, for example, a mess corporal would report on a commanding officer. By 1963–4 it was clear that there was a real danger that the only institution capable of resisting Nkrumah by force would before long lose its effectiveness because both of this kind of penetration and of the assembly of forces capable of countering it. Whatever may have been discussed in private between two or three officers about the possibility of resisting the deterioration of the Army's national position, there is no evidence of any serious propositions being made before 1965. Virtually the only source of information on this question is Colonel A. A. Afrifa who claims[1] that the possibility crossed his mind in 1962 and was revived more practically only to be blocked by the suspicions of the counter intelligence organiza-ation in 1964.[2] After the 1966 coup claims to have been the initiators of proposals at an early stage were made by several prominent persons in the police and the Army: it seems likely that from time to time conspiratorial conversations took place between a number of people, but that these contained no practical substance until the final plans were laid.

The developments already described and other indications such as the tentative steps to militarize the workers' Brigade seemed to the Army a threat to its own professional existence and the Air Force and the Navy were equally nervous of what might follow. Suspicions mounted steeply in July 1965 when Generals Otu and Ankrah were abruptly retired from the two senior defence staff posts. There were, of course, plausible reasons why this should be done. Both had been in office more than three years, were about fifty years of age, and were im-

[1] Colonel A. A. Afrifa, *The Ghana Coup, 24th February 1966,* London, 1966, p. 85.
[2] Ibid., p. 96.

H

portant elements in the promotion block which in rapidly developed new armies is always an important cause of officer discontent. The Army had no great objections to Aferi and Barwah who were promoted to fill the vacant posts, but it was undoubtedly suspected that these two were regarded by Nkrumah as more loyal than their two respected predecessors. It is possible that they may have resisted the increasingly independent status of the P.O.G.R., but the basis for Nkrumah's preference for Aferi and Barwah is not clear. Of all senior Ghanaian officers, Barwah, a Mamprussi from northern Ghana, might seem to have cultivated a more thorough-going professional detachment than any other and thus developed an exaggerated loyalty to the C.P.P. establishment on the grounds that it was the *de jure* government. This is the simplest explanation of his career as it is known to outsiders and of his death on the morning of the coup, but his enemies in the service felt that his implication in politics was more sinister than this.

The threat to the integrity of the various elements in the Ghanaian élite combined with the President's rapidly declining foreign prestige and the economic chaos in the country arising from prestige spending to bring the situation to a head and precipitate a coup. Again until further written evidence is published there seems small reason to doubt the account given in Afrifa's book already referred to of the difficulties which he and others experienced in bringing themselves to the point of taking political action. They seem[1] to have been reinforced in their intentions by the overt relationships of some of the officer corps with the politicians even though they themselves benefited by the chain of promotions which resulted from the retirement of the two generals. Afrifa refers[2] to the fear that Nkrumah would order the Army to take independent action against Rhodesia and confirms his belief in 'a non-military

[1] Afrifa, op. cit., p. 100.
[2] Ibid., p. 104.

solution'. It is doubtful, however, whether the rank and file were as disconcerted by this as Afrifa implies by saying:[1]

> Among our troops Nkrumah became unpopular because of this. They realized that he was sending them to war without proper equipment and without adequate preparation. The moment they started complaining I knew that the days of the Convention Peoples' Party were numbered.

What is clear and obviously tenable is the view that the coup was not only the last resort against an unpopular government but also the only means, in the circumstances, of overthrowing Nkrumah. Afrifa's words[2] are categorical:

> Where there was no constitutional means of offering a political opposition to the one-party government the Armed Forces were automatically made to become the official opposition of the government.

This and the ripeness of popular discontent carried the select group of officers trained in the allegedly apolitical British tradition through the resistance of their own consciences, but only their own ingenuity and discretion enabled them to achieve surprise in an informer-ridden society in which customarily secrets were not kept. As far as can be ascertained there were three people only in the advance planning of the operation – Brigadier E. K. Kotoka and Major A. A. Afrifa in the Brigade Headquarters at Kumasi, and J. W. K. Harlley, the Police Commissioner. Colonel Albert Ocran, the Commander of the Accra garrison, was brought in in the final stages. Nkrumah's departure for Peking and Hanoi was chosen as the signal because it was probably rightly felt that his absence would make the coup easier and less bloody. On 23 February 1966 the battalion stationed in Tamale moved south to join

---

[1] Afrifa, op. cit., p. 105.
[2] Ibid., p. 31.

up with the remainder of the brigade in Kumasi under the pretext of practice troop movement in connection with a Rhodesian operation. This force moved against Flagstaff House and other key points in Accra in the early morning of 24 February and at the same time police units began to make arrests of selected ministers and officials. It seems likely that the bulk of the soldiers concerned did not know what was really happening until 4 a.m. on the morning of the coup when the exercise became an operation, nor is it clear exactly when General Ankrah and other key individuals were alerted to their new rôle.

In spite of the fact that the Commander of the P.O.G.R., Colonel Zanlerigu, had escaped immediate arrest by the Army and the police and had thus been able to alert the defence of Flagstaff House in time to disrupt with fire the convoy arriving from the North, the coup went through almost according to schedule. That this was the case was due largely to the total acceptance of its objectives, as they were revealed, by the armed forces. Of the senior personnel only Major-General C. M. Barwah was killed on the steps of his bungalow, apparently as the result of his own spontaneous reaction to rebellion against the established order. To the writer who used to know him and Hassan Katsina well, there is an obvious comparison with the incident in Northern Nigeria on 15 January 1966 when Major Nzeogwu asked the latter 'Are you for us or against us?' and accepted the affirmative reply, probably to regret doing so later. It may be, however, that Barwah's commitment to Nkrumah was more complete than required under the terms of the formal allegiance of an officer to his head of state.

Colonel Afrifa himself with a depleted detachment seized the Radio Station and by 6 a.m. on the morning of 24 February 1966 Colonel Kotoka was announcing[1] over the air to an alerted nation that 'The myth surrounding Nkrumah has been

[1] Afrifa, op. cit., p. 35.

broken'. Even though the concentration of troops in Accra was not yet completed headquarters was established at police headquarters and an effective revolutionary government with Ankrah at its head created. Fresh troops quite quickly eliminated the sporadic resistance of the security guards at Flagstaff House, though the last resistance was not overcome until the following morning. The stubbornness of the P.O.G.R. at Flagstaff House has been widely attributed to the presence of East European advisers but there has been a conspiracy of silence about these men if they were indeed present and became casualties in the fighting: this may be attributed to diplomatic requirements.

Within a brief time the whole superstructure of the Nkrumah régime collapsed in such a way as to demonstrate the unique degree to which even the Convention Peoples' Party had been dependent upon Nkrumah's own inflated personality and in another sense the continuity which the civil servants in the ministries had been able surreptitiously to sustain. Almost without a break the administration of the country was picked up by the National Liberation Council (N.L.C.) acting through these men.

The account so far given indicates the origins of the coup without perhaps explaining fully the motivation of its leaders. Resentment against Nkrumah's arbitrary actions, corruption and mismanagement had become compounded in a disillusionment with the whole political apparatus. The catastrophically rapid deterioration in a once prosperous country's financial situation in the nine years since independence and the consequent growth in unemployment had first become starkly apparent at the time of the budget of 1961. The rise in prices and the scarcity of foreign imported goods was apparent on all sides. It is not necessary to look farther than this and the gradual demeaning of the Army and its attempted infiltration by the C.P.P. to account for the coup, the objective of which was simply the deposition of Nkrumah with the complex implications which would stem from it. The inspiration of this step seems not only to have been personal and practical but genuinely, if naïvely, rooted in a belief among the officers concerned in liberal democracy as they thought it ought to be and as they felt that they had experienced it in Britain. For Colonel Afrifa Sandhurst was a great liberal institution 'that teaches that all men are equal'[1] and there is no reason to doubt his sincerity in saying this or to claim that he thereby demonstrates himself to be a stooge of the British, an Anglo-African in the sense despised in some quarters[2] as contributing unwittingly to a world wide counter-revolutionary movement.

The National Liberation Council as set up in February 1966 was generally held to represent the nation-wide support for the deposition of Nkrumah in ethnic, regional, and even religious terms. Ewe, Ashanti, and Ga peoples, the Volta, Central, Ashanti, and Northern regions were all represented, as were Roman Catholics, Presbyterians, Methodists, Anglicans, and Islam. The deliberate nature of the decisions leading to this composition has probably been exaggerated, but if so the result has been fortunate in its effect and there has been little evidence of subsequent fission along tribal lines. Only with this degree of national unity at the top could the major economic problems inherited from Nkrumah have been tackled. The decline in Ghana's economic situation from relative prosperity in 1957 with world credits of over £100 m. to near bankruptcy at the end of 1965 is a proven fact and unemployment and the scarcity of imported consumer goods made this apparent to the people at large. The N.L.C. was thus faced with two major problems out of which in the short term it was difficult to obtain much credit: the economy could only be stabilized by 'long-haul' methods and the transfer of power back to a civilian administration involved the delicate matter of the

[1] Afrifa, op. cit., p. 51
[2] cf. e.g. Bob Fitch and Mary Oppenheimer, *Ghana: End of an Illusion*, New York and London, 1966, pp. 6–10.

reconstruction of political life which the coup had temporarily terminated.

The leaders of the Ghana coup were no exceptions to the usual rule that military leaders intervening in politics rarely have preconceived policies which they intend to apply. Essentially such groups begin by administering rather than governing: they are caretakers whose initial intention is often to end a trend of which they do not approve and to provide the framework within which government can be enabled to set off on a fresh course. They are not likely to have plans for widespread social change and the effect of their seizure of power may be virtually to wipe the political and constitutional slates clean.

The immediate post-revolutionary state of the successor government is the political equivalent of that of the new born babe. In it the functions of government are reduced to the minimum compatible with the survival of the social organism and the extension of political control throughout it from the initial stage of mere existence.[1]

The Ghanaian leaders were fortunate in that the collapse of the Convention Peoples' Party left virtually intact the departmental organization of the Ministries and the well-trained and experienced civil servants who headed the Civil Service within them.

The first phase of the post-coup administration was predictably a condemnation of the corruption and maladministration of its predecessor – those facts were its *raison d'être*, but even in his first major speech, a radio broadcast four days after the coup, General Ankrah stressed the intention of returning to genuinely democratic practices. He also said that the new government would resist all actions aimed at the undermining of the integrity of other African states and would cultivate a genuine non-alignment in foreign policy. To the

[1] Peter A. R. Calvert, 'Revolution: the Politics of Violence', in *Political Studies*, vol. 15, no. 1, February 1967, p. 11.

critics of military régimes as essentially reactionary symbols of a counter revolution this claim to non-alignment has seemed to be in practice a realignment in that, perhaps inevitably, help in a difficult situation has come most readily from Britain and the United States.

The first weeks and months of the new administration involved the dismantling of the complex ramifications of the old régime. While Nkrumah's opponents held in prison under the Preventive Detention Act were released *en masse*, political parties were banned and politicians and administrators with known C.P.P. affiliations were arrested and placed in protective custody pending a screening procedure which was, on the whole, operated with a reasonable sense of urgency. An important and not well publicized category of those arrested has consisted of those recruited for Nkrumah's President's Own Guard Regiment and elements of what have been described as his secret army. The comparative smoothness of the administrative transition must be largely attributed to the civil service (and perhaps the police) in their handling of the day-to-day affairs of the country. Positive steps were taken to eliminate corrupt elements from the bureaucracy at all levels and the more obvious causes of friction between the different elements of the élite. The same applied also to the judiciary which, however, required more reconstruction resulting from its perversion by the Nkrumah régime.

An interesting feature of the N.L.C.'s activities during 1966 was its largely successful handling of the Press and the academic sector of society. The popular newspapers, simply given fresh editorial control, changed their allegiance overnight while other journals like the *Legon Observer* began to publish considered criticism of the régime which like the more destructive comments of some university staff have on the whole been taken in good part by the N.L.C. This is perhaps the clearest indication of the genuine nature of the N.L.C.'s desire to return to civilian rule because the academics have been the strongest

champions of this course. They, with other elements in the
élite, have assisted with the commissions of inquiry and more
especially those charged with planning a new constitution and
the restoration of political life.

Immediately after the February coup in 1966 daily life in
Ghana returned to the genuinely relaxed atmosphere observed
by visitors as prevailing in the period immediately after independence in 1957. It was possible to move freely round the
country, hear the frank opinions of many people and to obtain
fairly rapid decisions from the bureaucracy. The evidence
suggests that post-coup optimism about the stability of
Ghanaian society, if not about its economic future, caused
security precautions to be relaxed to a dangerous point. So
clear was the absence of any substantial intertribal or regional
conflict among the leaders that the special vulnerability of
all revolutionary régimes to being overthrown by force was
ignored. It was not the need to rediscover a basis for legitimacy that was unrecognized but the practical dangers.
Thorough precautions were apparently taken to insulate the
State against the activities of the exiled president in Guinea.
As his presence there has become an increasing embarrassment
to his host so the danger from that quarter seems to have
diminished. Nevertheless all C.P.P. men who accompanied
Nkrumah on the critical Asian excursion and who have returned to Ghana have been very carefully screened. Others
who held official positions before 1966 without being obviously
implicated in the malpractices of the régime have, like Major-
General Nathan Aferi, been found relatively remote and,
therefore, isolated appointments overseas – General Aferi was
posted as Ambassador to Mexico, an appointment which he is
said to have accepted with some reluctance. This kind of
humane and essentially just treatment seems to be a characteristic of the régime in Ghana and Sierra Leone: if eventually it
were to prove unmerited in an individual case it would undoubtedly be castigated as overgenerous.

The ease with which Kotoka and Afrifa originally marched on Accra should have alerted them to the dangers which even a small dissident but cohesive body might hold. In such circumstances the carefully cultivated cohesion of the leadership élite might easily be disrupted. In the event, just over a year after the original coup an amateur counter-coup came near to success and in the process caused the death of General Kotoka. This counter-coup has generally been described as not essentially political and as arising from the discontent of junior officers. In so far as its motives are at all clear it might be classified as primarily an inter-generational conflict of the kind which is prone to emerge in rapidly expanded armies when promotion prospects eventually decline. The probability that the N.L.C. would, while restoring the standing of the Army in the community, not indulge in excessive expenditure on defence led to the conclusion that the career prospects of junior officers would be static for a substantial period. The promotion block and perhaps the zealous endeavours of the N.L.C. to balance the interests of the various public services, especially the Army and the police, were likely sources of the grievances which inflamed Lieutenants S. B. Arthur and M. Yeboah and 2nd Lieutenant E. Osei-Poku to action on the morning of 17 April 1967.

Arthur was acting commander of the Reconnaissance squadron based at Ho in the Volta Region. This unit with its light armoured cars was able to advance on Accra during the night without warning and attack Flagstaff House, the residence of the General Officer Commanding Defence Forces, General Kotoka, Osu Castle, the seat of government, and the radio station. The detachments achieved considerable initial success especially at Flagstaff House and the radio station and among the remainder of the Accra area there was almost total confusion. The only factors which saved the N.L.C. were the curious lack of persistence on the part of two of the rebel leaders once certain objectives had been achieved, and the total lack of organized purpose. For some hours on the day following the attempt, before the rebels were rounded up, there was a vacuum rather like that which prevailed after the mutiny in Dar es Salaam in January 1964. The confusion was increased by the dawn radio announcement of the setting up of a new council consisting of Lieutenant-Colonel J. Y. Assasie, Majors S. M. Asante, and R. A. Achaab. The real involvement of these three in the coup in even the most marginal way is highly questionable. Achaab, for instance, who comes from Navrongo in the Upper Region, had served with a reconnaissance squadron almost all his career and was known for an exceptional detachment on political matters, was actually held under duress by Lieutenant Arthur the coup leader in the operations room at Burma Camp. Assasie and Asante were both in Accra incidentally in connection with a promotions examination.

At the subsequent trial of Arthur, Yeboah, and Osei-Poku details of the sequence of events duly emerged. The original failure to resist the detachments from Ho was not altogether explicable nor was the behaviour of the members of the N.L.C., except General Ankrah and Brigadier Afrifa, who was in Tamale. The fact that there was a Reconnaissance regiment guard at Flagstaff House on the night in question helped to explain the easy access which was achieved there, but the lack of questioning at the radio station is not easy to understand. No member of the N.L.C. emerged as a rallying point for a counter-attack and there seems to have been little attempt to warn each other once the initial attack on Osu Castle had begun. If the same sort of vague chaos had not also characterized the rebel leadership – one of them was reported as having gone off to sleep with a girl-friend at the crucial moment – more of the N.L.C. leaders might have been lost.

The murder of General Kotoka had grave implications for the Council's effectiveness which it subsequently managed to weather. Lieutenant Arthur's grievances – and only his were clearly formulated – consisted primarily of a conviction that the N.L.C. members were 'feathering their nests' as the politicians had done before. In particular, their promotions to higher rank were seen as selfish and arbitrary acts. He also appears to have been vaguely resentful about the continuance of the economic crisis. There was also the possibility of a personality defect involving a Napoleonic type of megalomania in that he was a small man clearly carried away by his first experience of authority as an acting commander. He wanted, he said at his trial, to 'make history' by being the first lieutenant successfully to organize a coup. Whether he was in any way connected with 'The League of Young Army Officers' which had been issuing leaflets attacking corruption and the influence of the police in the N.L.C. was not demonstrated at his trial. The attempted coup did, however, bring out into the open the rumours of intertribal strife. Even though all the officers who died in the rising were Ewe and in spite of street corner gossip to that effect in Accra, the existence of an Ashanti-Fanti plot was effectively denied. There has been no significant resurgence of tribal tension in Ghana since, though Brigadier Afrifa has reminded the country of the danger. At the same time there was no evidence of a close connection between the coup leaders and ex-President Nkrumah.

The N.L.C.'s survival of this threat may have helped to clear the air and in the long run strengthened its position in more than one respect, but its immediate harsh reactions damaged its domestic and certainly its international image. After a very hurried investigation Lieutenants Arthur and Yeboah were convicted and executed by firing squad in public: heavy prison sentences of up to forty years were passed on other members of the reconnaissance squadron who had been implicated. The shock lay in the fact that under the Nkrumah régime men had been sentenced to death but apparently never executed. In fairness, however, it must be said of the N.L.C.'s actions that an administration which seizes power by force can only maintain its authority by ultimate severity. Nevertheless, the prospect of a succession of governments each endeavouring to find a basis for legitimacy and executing its predecessors and violent opponents is not one which Africa can afford. By comparison 'the general post' of senior armed forces commanders on the basis of their responsibility for the deficiencies of those below them was in an almost excessively civilized tradition. The commanders of the Army and the Navy were soon in Washington and London respectively as defence advisers to their government's missions.

In many respects, however, the attempted counter-coup did not alter radically the redevelopment of the country by the new administration. Immediately after the original coup took place it was frequently said that the real test for the N.L.C. would come when, in the course of drastic economic overhaul, it had to turn its attention to the security services on which it was itself based. The size of the regular Army and the police have been maintained, certainly not reduced, but there have not been any signs of lavish re-equipment. The order for the modern frigate under construction in Britain has been cancelled. Attempts to persuade the British Government into the unprecedented generosity of a gift of army uniforms and boots to re-kit the tattered soldiery run down by Nkrumah failed. Nevertheless the links with Britain as well as Canada and the United States have been strengthened. The emphasis has been on basic weapons, radio communications equipment, and vehicles, and training assistance has had a high priority. In January 1968 there was announced an exchange arrangement whereby two companies from each of a Ghanaian and British infantry battalion would visit the other country to gain experience of training in different climate and terrain. Many more officers have been to the United States for advanced training than was previously the case. The peripheral forces, not only the P.O.G.R., which had tended to rival the traditional security forces have been disbanded.

The extent to which Ghana has become a military régime is disputable. It is true that the Army was at an early stage given the arbitary power of arresting persons thought to be engaged in subversive activities and thereby might have attracted some of the dislike directed against the previous régime, but it appears to have used this unenviable authority with restraint. A reasonable discretion also seems to have characterized the actions of the regional administrations. Whereas under Nkrumah, Ghana was administered by Regional Commissioners who were in the end generally politicians nominated by the central caucus of the C.P.P., since 1966 regional committees of administration have been established with a senior military or police officer as chairman and also, in effect, garrison commander. The gradual separation of this administrative function from any aspect of military command is a first step towards the re-establishment of a civil administration in these circumstances.

The need for austerity in the handling of public expenditure stemmed directly from the debt of about £300 m. which the N.L.C. inherited in 1966. They have endeavoured to cut back on expenditure by closing down extravagant and futile state industries sometimes before the plant was even completed: such action was taken with the atomic reactor for which the Russians had provided substantial assistance because of the cost and the drain on scarce technical manpower which it involved. Basically, however, the administration has been concerned to attract aid and investment and to find means of honouring its obligations by rescheduling the international debts incurred by Nkrumah. Up to February 1968 three international conferences of Ghana's trading partners had been held to secure for her short-term loans to cover the balance of payments deficit.

The initial objective of endeavouring to cover all expenditure by current earnings proved unrealistic. Servicing of the debts was so considerable a task that the country could not have done this and survived economically or politically. The main implication would have been a cut back in economic growth which would further have raised a dangerous level of un-employment. The standing of the military régime was, however, such that the number of developed European and North American countries willing to be involved in negotiations in-creased at each meeting. By February 1968[1] the Netherlands, Norway, and Switzerland had joined a group which was pre-pared for the first time to consider certain kinds of development project such as rice development and palm oil plantations in spite of the fact that the time when Ghana would be able to manage normal repayment of debts was not yet foreseeable. The hope is that this small assembly of nations will become a 'consultative group' willing to pledge loans or grants for an agreed development programme. This is a measure of the im-provement in Ghana's economic condition since the coup. A balance of trade deficit of $116 m. in 1965 was transformed into a surplus of $24 m. in 1967[2]: this was achieved largely by a dramatic cut in the imports of consumer goods. At the same time, however, the heavy drain involved in the payment of interest on debts continued along with very sluggish growth of private and public capital. Much of this difficulty was due to external difficulties such as the rising costs consequent upon the Suez Canal closure and the dock strike in Britain. On the basis of the direct internal evidence, however, the policies of the National Liberation Council clearly achieved their main objective of restraining expenditure, though they had at the same time inevitably to compete with falling revenue from import duties. The International Monetary Fund report cir-culated in February 1968 spoke of 'the impressive progress which Ghana has made towards achieving one of the main objectives of its programme: namely, the restoration of mone-tary and price stability'. The National Liberation Council had

[1] *West Africa*, No. 2647, 24 February 1968, p. 212.
[2] *West Africa*, No. 2648, 2 March 1968, p. 244.

effectively controlled internal demand and provided a realistic basis for improvement and development.

In general economic terms then it may be said that the actions of the military régime in Ghana justifies its apparently rather naïve claims in overthrowing Nhrumah. It appeared to act in the public interest, to adopt sensible policies of retrenchment and to be aware of the dangers of a fresh decline into corruption. In this respect and in its apparently sincere search for a civilian alternative the Ghana administration demonstrated its good faith, but as military régimes are prone to do, it did show authoritarian tendencies from time to time. In spite of a deliberate attempt to re-establish a free Press in 1966, which Brigadier Afrifa frequently exhorted to be fearless, sensitivity to criticism of its policies eventually led the N.L.C. to interfere with that freedom. Ironically this occurred in defence of a sound economic action. Four editors of government-owned newspapers were dismissed for attacks on the N.L.C.'s agreement with Abbott Laboratories of the United States. This firm was, on good grounds, given preferential tax and import duty concessions together with a monopoly of official pharmaceutical supply until 1973 in order to enable it to salvage the organization set up by Hungarians during the Nkrumah period. The superficial charges of contributing to American neo-colonialism in the same way as Nkrumah had sold out to the Russians and East Europeans incensed the N.L.C. and the four editors concerned were dismissed. The Council's irritation at the attempt by journalists, not fully informed, to frustrate a plan of national importance was understandable, but it underestimated the importance of freedom, as opposed to economic policies, in the minds of most Ghanaians: it was the restoration of freedom which justified the coup of 1966 and in denying it on this occasion the N.L.C. was not only spoiling its own remarkably amiable image but weakening its fundamental *raison d'être*.

In foreign policy as well as internal economic policy the

N.L.C. has tended to retrench. Nkrumah's meddling in the affairs of other states and his attempts to subvert them were clearly anathema to the new leaders. His Pan-African ambitions and increasingly indiscriminate association with the Communist states were renounced in favour of more traditional policies based on the reconstruction of Western ties including the Commonwealth association: in this way a degree of neutralism has been restored. Initially this involved some deterioration of relations with Eastern Europe, the breaking off of diplomatic relations with China and Cuba, and some hostility within O.A.U. from militant Pan-African states of which only Guinea as host to ex-President Nkrumah persisted for long. It would seem that the N.L.C.'s resistance to the use of force in international affairs goes deep, and this applied to the situation in Southern Africa as well as elsewhere. Though the N.L.C. are anxious for a solution of the Rhodesian problem, Afrifa's comments[1] on the purposelessness of futile intervention by force there have not been disavowed, and taken together with General Ankrah's own attempts to reconcile Biafra and Nigeria mean that Ghana today is an important force for peace on the African continent. Such behaviour tended to endear the Ghanaian administration to Britain and America and produce the tangible dividends of confidence in the form of aid. Disarray in militant Pan-African circles diverted the usual criticisms of such developments.

The basic political achievement of the N.L.C. has been to replace the dictatorship of Nkrumah and the C.P.P. with an administration relatively free of corruption and capable of holding up its head internationally. The Army, Police, and Civil Service have for the time reconciled the conflicting interests within the country basically because they are the only representative institutions in the general sense. The problem of creating national consciousness and pride has been tackled in a manner tending to reverse the trends of the Nkrumah régime,

[1] Afrifa, op. cit., p. 104

I

but still maintaining the objective of national unity. The Centre for Civil Education under Dr K. A. Busia is one instrument for achieving this which deliberately eschews the methods employed by Nkrumah's labour and youth organizations. The trades unions and the universities have been encouraged to develop their independent contribution to national evolution untrammelled by political party interference. The régime will, however, be judged eventually by its degree of success in permanently transferring power back to civilian control and in reconstructing the political life of the country. Almost from the first the nation of a rewritten constitution was discussed and full powers were given to the Constitutional Commission to write it. What is more this commission was instructed to seek means of involving public participation in the process. Early in 1968 after more than one year's work the Commission under the chairmanship of the Chief Justice presented its recommendations which were supplemented by the work of a separate Electoral Commission.

The constitutional recommendations reflected clearly the intention to transfer power and at the same time the fears of the commission's members about a reversion to earlier practices and the consequent dangers. The extent to which the proposals were influenced by the subconscious knowledge that if things went wrong the Army could and would intervene again earlier rather than later is, of course, hard to say: this is an aspect of what is perhaps the most important psychological consequence of unconstitutional action and intermediate rule by decree. The Constitutional Commission was, however, clearly determined to avoid a return to an executive presidency and proposed both a prime minister and a president, though the latter would be obliged to exercise control and supervision over certain departments of state which ought to be as independent as possible of the Government of the day. In this and other rôles he would be supported and advised by a Council of State intended, it seems, to provide a formal means of achieving the sophisticated objective of oiling the machinery of government. It would be the President's duty also to recommend to the National Assembly the names of the Prime Minister and other ministers for their approval, though all of the latter need not be members of the assembly. The proposals for the membership of the Assembly itself laid stress on qualifications ensuring the close ties of members with the constituencies represented. The recommendations together with N.L.C. decrees virtually eliminated the prospect of former C.P.P. officials or M.P.'s returning to formal political life. The exclusion of chiefs from seats in the National Assembly reflected the desire to recreate the image of a modern democratic state in a similar way to the arrangements for guaranteeing the impartiality of the judiciary and the control of the financial affairs of the State. Commissions and Councils would control the various public services and advise the President on their recruitment and functioning. Elaborate precautions were proposed to avoid abuses of the electoral system particularly in relation to unopposed candidates, a notorious problem during the Nkrumah period. The proposed constitution specifically prohibits the enactment of a Preventive Detention Act, and the establishment of a one-party system. The consideration of the whole proposal should be by means of a constituent assembly representative of the people in a truly democratic sense.

The Proposals of the Constitutional Commission for a Constitution of Ghana (Government Printer, Accra) reflect clearly the dilemma not only of this particular commission, but of all who try to consolidate a revolution and to legitimize a régime, however respectable its intentions. The key question confronting them at every stage was how to start political life again without existing political parties. And by extension could even elections to a Constituent Assembly take place without facing this issue? Would it be possible to involve the best elements in the élite in government without involving them in the political or electoral process? The Constitutional Commission was clearly strongly influenced by British and American modes of thinking about the problem of the restraint of power. This body was clearly in a position not unlike that of the original authors of the American Constitution. The determination to divide and separate the powers was such that the restraints on the executive proposed might result in decision-making procedures too laborious for the needs of a developing country. On the other hand, the proposals that the President should be not less than fifty years of age and entitled only to one eight-year term of life and thereafter excluded from paid employment effectively reflected the singleminded determination of the commission. The proposed presence of 'the minority leader', the Chief Justice, and the G.O.C. Armed Forces in the Council of State was also significant. The independent Ombudsman and Auditor General would contribute to the checks on arbitrary power. Such a constitution when eventually put into practice could not guarantee itself the proper use of power: in spite of all the precautions it would depend markedly on the independent judgement and authority of talented individuals and on the successful political education of the public. The original Ghana constitution was workable but it was perverted and abused, by largely constitutional means.

The Ghana coup and its outcome over the first two years reflects clearly the power of the security forces especially in a small and compact country to take over the administration and to provide the opportunity for a reappraisal of the political situation. It illustrates the extent to which the colonial administrative institutions have interlocked with traditional elements to create the continuing structure of society. Stability in Ghana has involved a reversion to the known values of the colonial period and to the code of behaviour which goes with them. Nkrumah's creation of rival institutions, especially to the Army, was probably more important than the kind of idealism expressed by Colonel Afrifa in spurring the Army into action against his régime. The superior organization of the Army – to that of other institutions – enabled them to assume power. In Ghana they have made more progress than in many cases towards clearing up the mess left by the politicians, but to do so the officers have had to rule by decree like an old-time colonial government and in the same way to seek means of transferring power to new hands. In this search they have been fortunate in having the sympathetic understanding of the groups antagonized by Nkrumah – the intelligentsia, the traditional rulers, the former political opposition. Their confidence in releasing from restriction many important C.P.P. personnel may well have been justified by the unreal nature of that party when in power, but the question is whether in future the armed forces will be able to resist intervening again when a new political party in office pursues policies, especially a defence policy, which they are disposed to criticize. The legacy of the events of 24 February 1966 is not likely to be short-lived: legitimacy and a disinclination to revolutionary action are not easily re-established.

VIII · Foreign Military Assistance and the Political Rôle of African Armed Forces

Military aid to developing countries can take a number of different forms, the emphasis on which tends to change as independence is achieved and becomes a matter of past history. Basically, however, such aid consists either of equipment or training facilities or both. Equipment may be provided on widely differing terms of payment and may include the provision of training personnel or even of operators of sophisticated equipment, particularly planes or helicopters. Training may consists of facilities in the donor country provided on payment, free or at cut rates; alternatively training teams might be seconded or contracted to the recipient country either in an advisory capacity or actually to run an appropriate school or establishment. Various combinations of these arrangements have been tried particularly by the British and French in Africa. In the period immediately after independence, until 1961, for instance in Ghana, expatriates also often held command executive appointments even at a comparatively low level. Today Britain has exchange agreements with Ghana and Kenya for the training of subunits on each other's terrain. There is, however, no need in the context of this book to explore the technicalities of military equipment and training. The immediate concern is with the opportunities for contact and interchange which African armies have with other military cultures and the extent to which those contacts can have any bearing upon the conduct of army personnel, especially officers, and their attitudes to politics and to military intervention in them. To some degree this must depend on the rôle of the foreign military concerned in their own societies.

It is a reasonable assumption that officer training establishments at cadet, company commander, staff, joint services, specialist, or high strategic level are the most likely locations for meaningful culture contact to take place. Other training installations, whether at home or abroad, and relationships with individual officers and N.C.O.s from other forces may also clearly make an impact of a political or social nature, but the very length and particularly favourable physical conditions of the officer courses tend to make them especially important in this respect. The same may rarely be the case with opportunities for joint service with foreigners as occurred widely for African armies with the U.N. force in the Congo. It is possible that on all these occasions African military personnel may tend to acquire professional, social, and political attitudes as well as skills, particularly those of an administrative nature connected with command procedure. Sometimes international co-operation or the direct provision of new kinds of equipment may involve the acquisition of technical expertise, though in sub-Saharan Africa this has not often been the case above a fairly elementary level.

The effects of all this are bound to be speculative, but in individual cases exposure to other traditions may be both prolonged and intensive. To come under the influence or live within the framework of more than one foreign military establishment for a substantial period is likely to be a rare experience, but according to the policy of the government concerned about diversification of sources of assistance armed forces are likely to include individuals trained in more than one tradition. It is important in this context continually to bear in mind the fact that a military tradition is part of a total culture and cannot be wholly isolated from the society in which it has grown, and that at the same time military élites are part of more comprehensive national leadership élites and subject to the same influences and pressures. Indeed the closer integration of the military with their civil counterparts in new states where the total leadership group is small may be one of the most important reasons for the relatively greater frequency of military coups in developing than in developed countries. The differences between the political destiny of officer corps in old established and new states may well not lie in the presence or absence of scruples about military intervention in politics but in the fact that the opportunities and the reasons for intervening are more apparent. Colonel A. A. Afrifa's book *The Ghana Coup* not only provides a rare insight into the processes involved in the mind of a conscientious individual faced with the grave decision, but much evidence to suggest the, at any rate 'prima facie', influence of an external tradition.

The tradition to which Colonel Afrifa was exposed was, of course, that of the former colonial power. Unless there has been some abrupt break with the imperial past beyond a peaceful transition to independence, connections of this kind are likely for some years yet to have had the most profound effect. The practices and traditions of certain Western countries, notably Britain and France, were as widely spread as their empires. They are not only important in their own right where they continue today, but it is generally on top or in place of them that Russian, Chinese, Israeli, West German, Yugoslav, and other influences have to be exerted. The totality of the control of the imperial establishment over a colonial defence force cannot normally be matched in today's conditions in a 'free' state but has often been only slowly eroded by the new situation. It is, therefore, important to establish the extent to which foreign aid even in these seemingly ideal conditions can affect the political orientation of armed forces, with the proviso that the inevitable nationalist reaction against imperial associations must always be borne in mind. In what follows the effect of British military influence in Africa is taken as the main example.

Non-intervention in politics is assumed to be a characteristic of the Western military tradition. Like most generalizations this assumption is only partially valid. Thus one can reasonably argue that since the revolution of 1688 Britain's armed forces have remained relatively apolitical; although they came near to intervening in politics in Ireland in 1914, they have not actually done so. But this does not mean that they – the officers corps, at any rate – have not had and expressed effective political opinions. The élite ethos of the British forces has as its counterpart in the corresponding American institutions an intense professionalism. In neither country has the Army become at any time a political faction nor actively intervened on behalf of a particular political group, but in both countries the leadership of the defence forces has exerted considerable influence on policy. Thus there is a clear need to be cautious in distinguishing between political and apolitical military legacies. Nor can the rôle of the armed forces in this connection be validly considered in isolation from the general political circumstances prevailing in a particular country.

The difficulties of generalizing on this question are well illustrated by the varied political records of armies originally trained predominantly by the British. In Pakistan, in the Sudan, and, most notably, in Ghana there have been military assumptions of power: in India and Malaya the armed forces have remained detached and entirely subordinate to the civil authority. In Burma where the British connection was not quite so strong the Army has set up a socialist régime. Thus different tunes can be played on what appear to be similar instruments. It is at least a reasonable assumption that the sociology of the armed forces, especially of the officer corps, rather than the source of its training, and the general nature of political movements within the country, are the most important determinants of military behaviour. In the African context, moreover, not even the exceptionally small size of the armed forces in relation to the population and of the military leader-

ship in relation to the total élite has proved of great significance.

Before attempting to compare and analyse the behaviour of
African armies since independence, it would seem appropriate
to examine the supposed residual effect of foreign training on
the individual officer. Most of such training takes place outside
rather than inside the country of native origin: officer cadets
who do long courses in Britain, for instance, spend up to three
years in alien surroundings: in most other well established
countries a longer period of training for potential regular
officers prevails. If they are fortunate such young men return
to their own lands conditioned by a lengthy existence within a
closed institution of a totally different culture. The speed of
their reabsorption into their own society will obviously vary
and may in a few cases never be totally effective.

Chinua Achebe, the Nigerian writer, in *No Longer at Ease*
has described brilliantly the process as encountered by a young
civil servant with a western university education. The army
officer is to some extent protected against his own society by
life in a military camp which may very well retain at any rate
the superficial forms that prevailed in the colonial era. It is
commonplace to remark on the continuing resemblance to the
British Army of the forces of recently independent states. The
exaggerated respect for custom and the continuing ritual of the
officers' mess certainly have something like their original
meaning in the well established environment of the Indian
Army, but it may be doubted whether this is so in forces where,
in scale and duration, the tradition is much more tenuous. In
any case, even in Britain, the influence of the mess and the
instinctive loyalty of officers to one another and to the regiment is waning. Early marriage is a potent factor in weakening
the influence of the central institution to the extent that it
often appears today deserted and neglected. What is more, the
political impartiality which is so highly valued is neither directly inculcated nor discussed and may, in fact, not be ap-

parent from the tone of normal social conversation about the national scene. At the same time, military trainees from overseas tend, for their part, like other overseas students, to maintain political contacts with their own countries.

The passing down of a military tradition is, therefore, a specific form of cultural transfer which cannot easily be effected. It is not generally appreciated that any developed country involved in military assistance has no alternative but to offer the best by its own standards. Tailor-made courses specially designed to suit under-developed conditions would automatically incur the charge of discrimination, and the allegation that they were in some way second best. At the same time the desire of the independent recipient not to appear to be committed is liable to be underestimated. The tendency of Tanzania some years ago to 'shop around' from Holland to China and Canada to West Germany for training assistance has to be seen in this light. The continued preference for Britain and the Commonwealth as sources of military aid among Commonwealth new states is probably an indication of their relative disinterestedness, but the implicit apolitical tradition is really at variance with the ethos of one-party states which essentially want committed armed forces. President Nyerere wrote in the London *Observer* for 3 June 1962 that 'our conception of the President's office is obviously incompatible with the theory that the public services are and ought to be politically impartial'. This view has been reinforced and reiterated many times since. There are several African states today where lack of political enthusiasm might be regarded as tantamount to treachery, though it may be that the so-called one-party state is itself only a transitional phase.

Another factor working against the consolidation of a foreign military tradition is the strength of the family connection, which is invariably the centre of social activity and obligation, however much a few exceptionally sophisticated members of the local élite may seek individually to break it.

This in itself has already tended in West Africa to confine the regiment's influence to a formal working and ceremonial rôle. Officers with heavy and far-reaching family commitments often try to opt out of what is, after all, in the first instance an additional, and then an apparently irrelevant, expense. The political and the family factors combine to limit outside cultural influences and for the individual total acceptance of these influences can invite the suspicion of colleagues. Mode of dress, way of life, attitudes to women – all these can be regarded as betraying too complete an assumption of another set of values. This does not preclude the emergence of 'been-to' cliques or a response to particular situations conditioned by foreign experience; some young Tanganyikan officers trained in Britain were reported during the mutiny in January 1964 as having remained loyal to their commanders and having been treated as in the same category by the disaffected men. But foreign training seems to involve no guarantee of consistency of political behaviour: the facts that India's and Malaya's officers have remained apolitical, Pakistan's, the Sudan's, Ghana's, Nigeria's, and Sierra Leone's the reverse, bear repetition. Clearly local political and social circumstances are more important than foreign influences.

This relative unpredictability of effect means that the motives for providing foreign aid are less important than they might be if it were easily possible to realize intentions. It is a fair but no longer an unchallengeable assertion that American professionalism and the British élite ethos tend to assist the maintenance of political stability. Will Communist aid from Russian or Chinese sources do the same? It seems likely that a few well indoctrinated individuals may acquire key positions but in general direct political training is as likely to wear off as quickly as that which is indirect and informal. Perhaps indeed, the resentment which intense political instruction generates will create contrary prejudices. The evidence in Africa so far is that Western assistance needs to be self-effacing and genuinely disinterested. It may be that France has yet to reap the real disadvantages of maintaining formal defence links with her former dependencies too long. At the same time President Kenyatta's rejection in 1964 of a consignment of Russian arms as obsolete – which they were – was a sign that the same rules can apply to both sides in the struggle for influence. It is clear that, while developed countries have a duty to meet the legitimate security requirements of new states, at the same time they must avoid providing the ingredients of a dangerous local arms race. Fortunately it can reasonably be claimed that there is only one point in Africa where interests external to the continent are really parties to local rivalry. This is in the Ethiopia–Somalia–Kenya triangle, where American military aid to the first has exceeded that to all the rest of Africa put together and where the Soviet Union is assisting the second to a rapid, and for the size of the country, massive expansion of its armed forces. The problem is complicated by uncertainty about the future of French Somaliland. Other new African states themselves have to judge between the advantages of the positive neutrality achieved by varying the sources of training and supply, and the confusion likely to be caused within armed forces by the mixture of three or four traditions. The objections of senior Ghanaian officers in 1961 to sending cadets to Russia were largely due to this and related fears.

It is against the background of these general considerations that the development of military-political activity in Africa must be seen. The sophisticated nature of the military rôle in some South East Asian countries is partially due to the long approach to independence. In Africa military establishments are generally small and the achievement of independence has been so quick that there has been little opportunity for attitudes to crystallize. To point for instance to the mutinies in East Africa in January 1964 as forerunners of a grand intervention in politics by African armies is to magnify their significance: as we have seen they seem to have been largely due to grievances connected with pay and promotion complicated by racial tensions. The immediate theory that the Tanganyika mutiny was partly due to the frustrated ambitions of young Sandhurst-trained officers, who had acquired the habit of regarding themselves as élite, was soon discounted. The mutineers in Kenya were dealt with most sternly and in each case (and in Zambia also as a forestalling measure) a review of pay and allowances followed. In Uganda according to the latest evidence mishandling of grievances by an African minister had served to inflame a delicate situation between the races. It may be that in all these countries there was confusion in the soldiers' minds between the new authorities and the old; for instance it would not be surprising if those enlisted to fight Mau Mau in the 1950s were not altogether clear as to their proper allegiance faced with a predominantly Kikuyu Government. It is a measure of the statesmanship of Jomo Kenyatta and some of his moderate supporters that a widespread malaise in the security forces has not developed from this cause. What has been of questionable merit both in Kenya and Tanzania is the subsequent encouragement of youth wing members of the ruling political parties to enlist. Sooner or later some African politicians will have to decide whether they really want a people's army not unlike the Chinese pattern or to choose between the various élite systems otherwise available to them: national military institutions as they eventually emerge are likely to be adaptations of systems which exist elsewhere.

Comparisons between events in East Africa and those in French-speaking West and Equatorial Africa are tempting but misleading. France made in 1960 a series of formal defence agreements with the Community countries. They referred specifically to internal security and in a sense gave the French Government the discretion to intervene in certain circumstances. Though no deliberate decision on principle ever seems to have been taken, a useful convention appears to have sprung up to the effect that whereas a mutiny might justify active assistance to an established, legitimate government, a genuine popular rising would not. Broadly speaking this convention can be said to have been adhered to in the cases of Togo, Dahomey, and Congo (Brazzaville). In the Togo Republic a few discharged veterans combined with the tiny army to over-throw President Olympio's régime and incidentally, probably accidentally, to assassinate him. In the Congo, French troops in substantial numbers remained uncommitted in the vicinity of Brazzaville while the Abbé Fulbert Youlou was forced out of office. Nor yet did they take any steps to interfere when in Dahomey an army rising involving about eight hundred men led initially to the disintegration of President Maga's Government and to a first interlude of military rule. It is true that in Gabon French 'neutralism' was not maintained: there metro-politan forces played an active rôle in the restoration of President Mba. But it was perhaps no coincidence that this incident took place in the month following the three East African governments' appeals to Britain for assistance, and probably the French decision, which was of a kind which now seems unlikely to be repeated, was more influenced by the question of France's prestige in relation to Britain than by her concern for the mineral wealth of Gabon. There are obvious dangers to the interests of outside powers if they voluntarily make a choice of sides in minor conflicts of this kind which may well be a feature of the African scene for years to come. It will be as well if they can maintain the rôle of onlookers, especially as it is less likely that the military will actually seize power than simply seek, in conjunction with other forces in the com-munity, to transfer it from one set of hands to another. They are more likely to be the agents of current dissidence than the upholders of a consistent political philosophy.

For the military to emerge as a permanent power group they need real professional cohesion, such as is unlikely where 'localization' of the bulk of senior ranks is recent, and a near monopoly of technical 'know how'; but while these factors, combined with arms, transport, and a separate communications network and a reputation for administrative efficiency, may bring military governments into power, political circumstances in Africa, and especially the small size of the military forces there, do not seem appropriate for their long survival. We should guard in this connection against too sweeping assertions based on events in Nigeria and Ghana. While in Nigeria the Africanization policy of the imperial power may have had some bearing on the conflict, this is surely a case where tribal and regional affiliations have succeeded in obliterating the effects of foreign example with regard to political participation. In Ghana, on the other hand, there may be superficial grounds for feeling that the political views of the leaders of the coup were strongly influenced by the British connection. Certainly Colonel Afrifa's book is full of pronouncements about democracy and his experience of its fruits at Sandhurst and in Britain generally. But to regard the coup against Nkrumah as a neo-colonialist victory for those whom some term 'the Anglo-Africans' involves distortion and over-emphasis of the facts. Closer examination of published statements shows the political ideas of the organizers of the coup to consist of the sort of generalized democratic sentiments which opponents of any oppressive régime would be likely to express. More significant is the clear crisis of conscience which the decision to intervene involved for men like Kotoka and Afrifa.

The unknown factor in these and other difficult situations is the extent to which countries with communist ideologies may influence the behaviour of the armed forces. In Indonesia there was for years a tug-of-war between an air force in which Russian influence was strong and an army in which American training elements predominated. But as Russian institutions tend increasingly to generate their own élite systems it may be that the distinction between what they and the West have to offer in this respect is becoming blurred. The importance of the Chinese bid for influence in Africa may eventually lie precisely in the Chinese adherence to the concept of a people's army which has a definite appeal to the leadership of an undeveloped state. The sudden decision early in 1965 by China's state council to abolish all military ranks may misleadingly have appeared to confirm her suitability to provide assistance. The fact that in China this was a victory for those who wished to adhere to the guerilla warfare tradition of the liberation over those who urgently desired the country to become a modern military power could in itself be a recommendation to new states with an exiguous defence budget and preoccupied with, for instance, the subversion of Rhodesia, the Portuguese territories, and South Africa. What they will not perhaps immediately recognize is that this success for China's old guard cannot be more than temporary, and even such influential friends will probably not in the long run protect political leaders against the hostile 'politicization' of their armies in another way.

There are few of the new states that have placed their regular forces in danger of manipulation from a single external source. Tanzania, in allowing the establishment within her boundaries of training camps for guerilla fighters manned by Russians, Cubans, and Algerians, is clearly following a policy which carries its own risks of subversion: but most of the African countries are like her seeking to demonstrate their nonalignment and to assert positive neutralism by accepting assistance from diverse sources. Such a policy is likely to create problems for the armed forces, perhaps in the form of cliques of officers educated in a variety of traditions. Military aid before independence was, as has been stated, total: training of officers and other ranks at all levels, equipment, technical assistance, and even expatriate commanders were all forthcoming. From the political point of view training aid is undoubtedly the most important as soon as expatriates in executive positions have been dispensed with.

K

A distinction must be drawn at this point between foreign military assistance directly associated with the strategic interest of the donor and that which is less obvious in its motivation. American and Australian aid to South Vietnam comes into the first category, as did Britain's to Malaysia in the confrontation with Indonesia. It is perhaps worth noting that, in Africa, United States grant aid is largely directed to those countries like Ethiopia, Libya, and Morocco where the Americans have or have had bases. Elsewhere it may be said to be provided in order to win friends and influence people, by assisting the establishment of stable governments, and generally to increase the internal security capability and ensure the free world orientation of small states. Harold A. Hovey in his book on military aid[1] has emphasized this attitude while at the same time recording the decision of Congress that assistance to new African states should be for 'internal security and civic action requirements only': for some the effect of this decision may be spoilt by Mr Hovey's footnote 'of course, there is nothing about United States-provided bullets which makes them useless for external defense even though they were provided to meet internal security requirements'.

Sometimes a major power's interest in supplying military material is purely commercial, but this is rarely the case. What is clear is that the immediate objectives are infrequently achieved: the 'pay-off' when it occurs is only indirect. Foreign politics and diplomatic actions are not so easily influenced. Britain has military missions or Joint Services Training Teams in countries like Libya, Ghana, and Kenya. She tends to give major equipment only where, as in Libya, she has a direct strategic commitment. How far such gifts affect local policy is hard to say; probably in the last resort not at all, but they do induce a definite orientation of the military leadership concerned towards British methods of administration and con-

[1] Harold A. Hovey, *United States Military Assistance* (London, 1966), pp. 110–12.

trol. Their very professional cohesion may in the end give them the capability of military action. It is difficult as yet to trace to, for example, China in Congo (Brazzaville) any specific responsibility for the political behaviour of the Army there. Nor does Norway's training of the Ethiopian Navy have any apparent significance of this kind, but it may well be argued that the invitation to the Indians to retrain the Imperial Guard in that country after the 1961 rising and to man the Military Academy at Harar is based on the assumption that the Indian Army is safely apolitical. A parallel and now ironical assumption may be supposed to have been behind Ghana's early termination of the arrangement for the training of a few officer cadets in Pakistan: the inference was that training in that environment after President Ayub Khan's establishment in power might lead to political consciousness among the young officers.

In one case, that of Israel, it is possible to detect that her notions of a citizen army carefully identified with the State and committed to national service projects have found positive favour in some quarters. A non-aligned state, untainted with imperialism but with Western technological advances at its disposal, clearly has advantages to developing countries. The influence of her traditions suitably fed into the armed forces, the youth organizations, workers' and women's associations may be actually formative of national consciousness in a unique fashion.

It seems, therefore, that foreign aid from specific sources has some influence on the political behaviour of embryonic armed forces, but that its direction is unpredictable. What is much more significant is the general effect of such assistance in the forms that it normally takes. In particular, the training of officers overseas creates a new and significantly large element in the educated élite of the country concerned, through which new ideas may easily enter from Europe and elsewhere. Similarly technological and technical qualifications and skills of all kinds are acquired, from degrees in engineering to the ability to maintain a simple internal combustion engine. With these also go standards of hygiene at one level and techniques of administration at another. It is obvious that the capacity to handle weapons is acquired and with it the means to power in small countries: more subtly, systems of radio and telephone communications enable military political action. It is very often foreign aid which gives to armies the power to intervene in politics, but the purpose of intervention is more likely to be determined by particular local conditions than by the influence of a source of assistance. In fact, the professional traditions of the major powers who provide the majority of aid, be it in Latin America, Africa, or Asia, are more likely to inhibit the development of partisan attitudes than to encourage them: that there is no consistency in the pattern of the military in politics is perhaps the best proof of this. From the cases here examined it is fair to assume that progressive military training under the auspices of a well developed power does inculcate professional standards of honesty, punctuality, service, and loyalty. These qualities of varying importance all relate to politics as to the military life: the evidence from Ghana, Nigeria, Sierra Leone, and certain of the Francophone countries is that this aspect of a foreign military tradition may have a bearing on the decision to intervene as may the corresponding development of a sense of national pride. Inevitably the behaviour patterns of young officers like General Gowon are influenced by the company they have kept. Their reluctance to operate politically may well as a result be genuine but the decision to act is likely to be activated by cruder considerations. The Sandhurst and St Cyr training and traditions cannot themselves be held responsible for the rash of military coups in Africa, but their 'alumni' have the kind of reputation which makes them acceptable, at least temporarily, as the agents of 'corrective' government.

IX · The Political Rôle and Motivation of the Military in Africa – an Assessment

Though each of the cases of military intervention in politics tells something of the situation and behaviour of the particular army within its own society, the problem of constructing valid generalizations, except of the widest nature, remains. This is due, as has been emphasized, to the proper need to treat each military institution as integrated into the social structure of its own society and not separated from it. In other words, sound generalizations are likely to be as much concerned with the political behaviour of the whole society as with that of the defence forces in particular. Nevertheless, the qualities of armies which so frequently make them the focus or the hinge on which political events turn when a society has reached a crisis point need to be analysed. For it is military deployment of these qualities or the exploitation of them by others which leads to intervention in politics.

The African examples already described are sufficient to prove that the size of armed forces in relation to the total population of a country has little bearing on their liability to intervene in politics. Though the nature of a subsequent military administration is likely to be considerably affected by the number of trained men in uniform available to play administrative parts, very few soldiers can, in the first instance, effect a coup especially if they are seeking primarily to transfer power from one group to another or perhaps simply to deny power to a potential tyrant. The first manifestations of the Togolese and Dahomeyan military in politics came into the former category and the revolution against Nkrumah in the latter. It is, of course, the possession of arms which gives them the capacity to do this. Arms, their use or very often only the threat to use them, are the *sine qua non* of military intervention, but though essential, they are only part as it were of an army's armoury when compared with any armed civilian group which might be secretly assembled. In most countries where any degree of development has taken place the Army and the Police have at least the rudiments of a communications system separate from that provided for the general public. In Lagos and Accra at the time of the coups command posts were set up at the police headquarters in order to exploit this advantage. Nevertheless radio, television, cable stations, and major telephone exchanges normally require to be taken over. Similarly the defence forces have their own transport, though as it happens the African countries concerned had very little military air transport at their disposal at the time of the coups described and appear to have made little use of what there was. Such technical 'know-how' as armed forces personnel possess is clearly important to the effectiveness of intervention, but in the cases concerned, as it happens, this expertise has not generally extended beyond basic knowledge of the operation of mechanical road transport, radio communications, temporary bridge building, and demolition. There have been problems connected with railway operation, water and power supply, but in each case liaison with the appropriate civilian staff has generally been good and sabotage by the withdrawal of expertise a factor of almost no importance. In Nigeria, as the situation has developed, the lack of trained pilots and aircraft engineers has led to the recruitment of highly priced foreigners, but at the time of the initial coups both in Nigeria and Ghana, it has been sufficient that the existing small air forces have been associated with the rebels. In Nigeria in January 1966 a Nigerian Officer, Lieutenant-Colonel George Kurubo, was appointed as Commander of the Air Force but this had no technical significance.

Administrative skills, however, have been more important. In both French- and English-speaking Africa the initial organizations and the day-to-day administrations in the post-coup phase have on the whole been impressive. Less efficient leaders, and one thinks here of the quality of men like the young Colonel Afrifa in Ghana, would have engendered bloodier situations in the first instance and rapidly deteriorating standards thereafter. The military governors in Nigeria all had some success in keeping the commercial life of the country going in difficult circumstances. The simple military administrative procedures with which such men were imbued have considerable advantages in the context of the relatively unsophisticated state structure of developing countries, but they also contain features which may in the long run constitute difficulties. The strictly hierarchical arrangement calls for the issue of exceptionally straightforward instructions from superior to subordinate, and the nature of the situation may require a greater latitude of discretion than these allow for. Similarly there may be a tendency to underrate the importance of consultation and thereby gradually to encourage the isolation of the leadership from the trends and nuances of opinion and attitudes at the lower levels of society. This is in any case encouraged as between the defence forces, other than the police, and the people by the segregated military way of life which the British and the French have passed on to their former colonies.

This segregation, however, is an important factor in making coups possible. The cohesion of a relatively homogeneous army – not, of course, that of federal Nigeria – owes a great deal to the fact that it is usually stationed round the country in a few largish units outside the towns and protected by readily accepted security arrangements against intrusion and against questioning about its actions. Thus the army camp, where the Army is not divided itself, provides a ready-made base for preparation, and operation and movements can be disguised, as in Ghana, under the cloak of operational training. The active co-operation of the police makes for an even stronger position, though if they wanted to act independently they would find that their distribution under junior officers in very small sub-units all over the country was a disadvantage. In armies created in the British pattern the dominance of an officer corps with an élite outlook used to exercising an essentially paternalist consideration for a whole social unit, with women and children actually on the camp, makes for even greater facility in developing cohesion. It can reasonably be claimed that an officers' mess in this tradition forms an almost ideal locale for conspiracy and the especial objection of Ghanaian officers to Nkrumah's attempt to insinuate spies into this exclusive institution deserves notice. In short, an army, unless tribal or other extraneous loyalties seriously interfere, is a cohesive, trained organization with recognizable and predictable patterns of allegiance which make the risks of plotting minimal, if the whole force of the Army is to be turned against the political apparatus. A remarkable feature of most African coups is the small number of people who were fully privy to the plans for intervention in the first instance and the extent to which they were subsequently able to rely on their colleagues to respond to their leadership at short notice. This indicates either individual leadership qualities of a higher order, or a combination of a close understanding of the mood of fellow soldiers with effective training in obedience to orders.

The qualities of an army which give it the capacity to intervene in politics, as outlined above, are, as it were, a form of reserve power existing within a state, the use of which is commonly regarded as unconstitutional or illegal. The term 'legitimate' as applied to military action under considerable political provocation would, of course, be misleading in that the consequence is often necessarily the establishment of a régime which then has to discover a new basis for constitutional legitimacy. The fact that the action taken is legally unconstitutional, though in some cases it might reasonably be regarded as in the defence of the constitution, is often disturbing to the military leaders responsible. The fact that General Ankrah tried to justify the Ghana coup, by claiming it was not unlike a traditional 'destooling' of an unsatisfactory chief, confirms the nervousness on this aspect clearly expressed by Colonel Afrifa in his book. 'A *coup d'etat*' he wrote[1] 'is the last resort in the range of means whereby an unpopular government may be overthrown. But in our case where there was no constitutional means of offering a political opposition to one party government the Armed Forces were automatically made to become the official opposition of the government.' This kind of reaction to political misdirection is likely to be strongest where the armed forces themselves feel threatened or neglected, and this feature is particularly clear from the history of events leading up to the Ghana coup in February 1966. In other cases failure to keep service pay and conditions abreast of those in other forms of employment or economies imposed on public servants generally have been contributory factors. Such steps, however, imply general economic difficulties in the country in question and it is tempting as usual to attribute to economic causes apparently inexplicable political phenomena.

Unsatisfactory economic situations, wide gaps in prosperity between social classes and financial mismanagement have been a feature of many countries on many occasions in history, but military intervention in politics is less widespread. Clearly the attribution of coups to economic causes must be approached with some caution. It may be that while in certain sophisticated states impending economic disaster leads to a demand for a national or coalition government, in others the Army is seen as the only means of firmly reconciling interests and co-ordinating the national effort when discord is dangerous to the whole fabric of society. This is a possible explanation for the relatively more frequent coups in developing than in developed countries,

[1] Afrifa, op. cit., p. 31.

but are the situations in which they take place significantly economic in their origin?

Certainly the governments of recently independent states have a strong interest in rapid economic development, for it is on this that their reputation rests once the euphoria of the initial nationalist triumph has worn off. Many of them, perhaps particularly in the Francophone African countries, are quickly enmeshed in attempts to maintain economic progress in state units which are not really viable. Others may simply not live up to their supporters' excessively stimulated expectations or be diverted into one form of mismanagement or another. Rising expectations are augmented by the development of an educational system which tends in particular categories to produce more manpower than can be appropriately employed. Ghana was a case in point and Nkrumah's Workers' Brigade a clumsy attempted solution. A climate of dissatisfaction over economic circumstances is likely to produce a desire for political change, but the only case of unemployment directly linking with a coup was in the Togo Republic where the discharged French African veterans staged the coup.

The Congo (Brazzaville) coup in which President Fulbert Youlou was deposed was attributable in some degree to union unrest combined with the presence in the capital of some thousands of unemployed youths. There the trades unions were a force behind the Army coup and without unduly stretching the imagination the Army might be seen as acting as an agent of the unions. In Dahomey also, in October 1963, a general strike was the background against which the transfer of power took place, but the strike had practically expended itself when other military and political factors came into play. Nevertheless the failure of successor governments including that of Soglo to tackle successfully the problems of economic development in such a way as to satisfy a broad band of the country's interests has proved a reason for continual politico-military activity. In the Central African Republic similarly a broadcast by the President on the economic situation which included among other things announcement of a deliberate reduction in French aid and a corresponding cutback on development projects was the signal. With a case such as this in the C.A.R., however, it is not easy to distinguish between factors affecting the sophisticated élite and those arousing the unskilled urban unemployed. Such subtleties as the effect of membership of the Central African Customs and Economic Union are not popularly inflammatory in themselves, but it is the close knit nature of many of the newer élite groups which could make these matters factors in bringing the Army into play. Threats to freedom of speech and liberty of action can readily find expression among officers via their contacts with educated minorities such as the trades union leadership, and austerity and restraint of union liberties commonly go together. One question is, however, the extent to which the Army sees the crisis in other terms: general experience in Africa suggests that the conservative training of officers inclines them to wish to defend the constitution rather than the economy. When an austerity budget and wave of strikes and demonstrations seemed to threaten violence in Upper Volta in the first week of 1966, Colonel Lamizana, as Army Chief of Staff, took over 'to safeguard republican and democratic institutions and avoid bloodshed'. He managed to secure the support of the trades unions partly by cancelling a wage cut.

In countries like Nigeria where the economy has from the first seemed reasonably soundly based, it would nevertheless be possible to paint a picture of labour unrest and relate it directly to the causes of the coups. The relationship, however, in such cases would appear circumstantial and symptomatic rather than fundamental. Such incidents as the threat of the unions to withdraw from the Morgan Commission on Salary Structure when proposals were published for a dramatic increase in the pay of Members of Parliament were no more than might normally be expected in any society, though the federal structure with its proliferation of ministers and elected members was particularly vulnerable to such criticism. When general considerations of pay increases and unemployment are in question, an important factor in two ways is the ability of the trades unions to unite and form a cohesive body for the purposes of exercising political influence – unity strengthens the chances of exerting pressure on the Government and makes communication with other dissident bodies, for example, in the Army more practicable. In the period before the January coup in 1966 in Nigeria, the unions were in a state of disarray and had failed effectively to protest against the 'rigged' election in the West. The military coup was initially popular with and tended to unite them but they could not claim to have done much to bring the administration to power. It is open to question to what extent rivalry for jobs between ethnic groups was responsible for the counter coup in July: it is likely that it helped to foment the deep resentment in the North at Ibo success in many fields, including for a few months even the achievement of political power.

The case of Ghana was different from the Nigerian situation in the sense that it was not so much failure to develop the economy positively which led to unemployment and a rise in the cost of living, as well as a fall in its standard, but the financing of prestige projects such as Ghana Airways in ways which undermined a prosperity which had been there for the taking. An austerity budget had caused a labour crisis in 1961 and some disquiet in the Army at the prospect of being used to break up a dangerous strike situation. The economic situation steadily deteriorated with rising prices and the disappearance of many imported consumer goods from the shops provoked complaints at the levels of informed society which also objected to the image of the country created by the party and presidential nominees in the key offices and in the state corporations. The question as to whether popular discontent is always economic in its origins arises here. Was it exploited by

the coup leaders or simply taken into account by them in as-
sessing their chances of popular support and overall success?
Afrifa scarcely mentions this factor but General Kotoka was
reported[1] as having said to a B.B.C. reporter 'We allowed him
(Nkrumah) to carry on so that the people could feel the pinch.
We gave him a long rope to hang himself.' This could be interpreted as signifying a cleverly calculated approach exploiting
economic discontent with ulterior motives or simply an *ex
post facto* justification for not having overthrown Nkrumah
at an earlier stage. But in 1966 the unions did not react strongly
to a budget, published on 21 February, which was similar to that
which had angered them in 1961 and the coup took place on
the 24th. There is no direct evidence that the timing of the
coup was related to the budget: Nkrumah's departure for
Peking and Hanoi seems to have been decisive. The powerless-
ness of organizations other than the Army to act against
Nkrumah was by this time recognized by the coup leaders.
The feeling that time was running out and that there would
soon be no opportunity left to overthrow the régime was itself
of some importance.

The main examples of military coups in Africa which have
been referred to indicate that, whether consciously or not, there
was no action without the prospect of popular support either
from the trades unions or just generally. Whether this is any
indication of the real social basis for revolution is, however,
highly questionable. A feature of African political development
has been the high degree of spontaneity, unpredictability, and
general volatility of political reactions at all levels. It is for this
reason as much as any other that it is unwise to set too much
store by an analysis of the finer points of these coups. Given
this and the concentration of power, generally in one party at
the national level, it is reasonable to expect that there will be
many occasions when a small number of opportunists backed

[1] *Africa Research Bulletin* – Political, Social, and Cultural Section,
February 1966, p. 466.

by arms will be able temporarily to take advantage of current popular sympathies. The tendency for the governments of new states not only to perform the political and administrative functions but to act as large-scale employers in state corporations and on projects tends to focus discontent. The fact that the military coups in question have had little impact on the fundamental economic and social structure of the states indicates that they are not revolutionary in the true sense and not to any degree an expression of the deprivation of any sections of society in basic terms.

Though economic discontents provide a backcloth conducive to the performance of military coups, the problems in this field are such that the same set are likely to continue for a long time with minor variations. A new régime can generally only offer palliatives for economic difficulties: of the military governments mentioned only that of Ghana with its relatively clear cut task has been able to make much headway. In other cases, it is just not feasible to achieve economic viability in a short period. The economic problems are, therefore, liable to become a threat to the new régime. The cycle of austerity budgets with cuts in capital expenditure and other economies is repeated and it is, in these circumstances, not easy to maintain an expensive military establishment. Restraints on its growth spoil career prospects and create discontents among those who in rapidly localized armies are likely already to be held up by a promotion block. This quickly results in the charge that the military administration is not living up to its claim to be an agency of reform and an attempted counter-coup, like that tried by young officers in Ghana, is then on the cards.

The charge of corruption and misappropriation is frequently made to justify military coups in Africa as elsewhere. The question is not whether it exists – it is clearly in many states rampant – but whether it is of any great importance in promoting such events. This again is a matter of political behaviour. In a poor community conspicuous expenditure is an incitement to protest and violence on the part of those who are deprived, but are relatively comfortably placed army personnel living in what were European residential areas necessarily affected by this? A blatant manifestation of extravagance at the time of an austerity budget is obviously impolitic and President Yameogo in Upper Volta seems to have disregarded popular sensitivities in this way. It may be that Chief Festus Okotie Eboh, Federal Finance Minister in Nigeria, would not have been selected for abduction and murder if his financial manoeuvres had not appeared unusually reprehensible. But reading the reports of the various commissions of inquiry into these matters in Ghana, one is left with an impression that, though the revelations are scandalous, this is almost a ritual exercise of justifying in another and conventionally accepted way an act which to most Ghanaians did not need any elaborate apologia. The trap lies in the danger that the new rulers will become known to have succumbed in however marginal a way to the same temptations. In Nigeria and Ghana, so far as can be ascertained, the degree of self denial has been such as to deserve admiration and on a par with the drives which have taken place with regard to punctuality, hygiene and generally orderly behaviour, and such other matters as are thought to be the overt signs of civilized modern society.

The general conclusion then must be that in a variety of circumstances with economic and other overtones military coups in Africa are usually about the distribution of power in society and to some extent about the proper status of the military within that society. There is also evidence that there is concern these days for the standing of the State in the eyes of the world, and that when things seem to go awry it is natural for the Army to step in because it is seen as patriotic by definition and possessed of unusual virtue and rectitude. The point at which the Army ceases to be the willing instrument of the Government of a newly independent state and takes over its powers may come when it feels threatened as an institution or when it is required to carry out policies which are unacceptable on behalf of politicians whose personal or public conduct is distasteful. All these elements could be observed at work in January and February 1966 in Nigeria and Ghana. The difficulties arise from trying to keep in power or to find a formula for a return to civilian rule. The basic problem is that military administrations take office because of the defects of particular politicians and once there may become convinced of their own general superiority in this respect. There has so far been one remarkable case, in Sierra Leone in April 1968, of a counter-coup of junior military personnel organized allegedly purely to facilitate the process of 'recivilianization', though there have, of course, been other cases of the succession of a military régime by a civil government.

The difficulty lies, it seems, in the process of deliberately organizing the transfer of power and the crux of it is, perhaps, in the revival of political parties. The banning of such parties has generally been seen to be an essential concomitant of military rule, but it is hard to see how without them genuine political life can be recreated. At the same time, the essentially 'holding' nature of a military government's function makes it unlikely that the process will begin again at a point of development very much different from that at which it was forcibly suspended.

In this matter of deliberate demilitarization the two most interesting cases are probably those of Ghana and Sierra Leone. The National Liberation Council in Ghana was undoubtedly greatly assisted by the widespread satiety with politics generated by Nkrumah and the C.P.P. and was, therefore, able to proceed with measured tread, though opinion within the Council seems to have varied about the relative need for haste: Brigadier Afrifa, consistently with his published professions of democratic principles, was from the first the most urgent. Preliminary steps were completed by the beginning of April 1968 when an interim Electoral Commissioner was appointed. This was itself a preliminary to the creation of a Constituent Assembly on a fully elective basis and it meant that the elections to the assembly might be themselves the major step towards a new political life whether parties were made legal in the interim or not. Disqualification from office, subject to a right of appeal for exceptional status, was prescribed for all those who had previously held office in the C.P.P. Ghana's dilemma was similar to that of Dahomey over the banning of former holders of presidential office from competing for the presidency anew. Such bans posed the question whether the military caretakers could possibly have created the circumstances in which a fresh start to political development was possible.

The Ghana Constituent Assembly as laid down provided for a detailed review by it of the proposals of a constitutional commission with their innumerable safeguards against a return to authoritarian rule. These proposals were by no means uncontroversial and provided, for instance, for Supreme Court jurisdiction over industrial disputes. No arrangements were made for the resolution of disagreement between the Constituent Assembly and the National Liberation Council itself and this is precisely the kind of situation over which any military government's determination to return to civil rule may falter. It was reasonable also to question the practicability, and, indeed, the validity of a referendum on top of the deliberations of a constituent assembly. It was certainly questionable how meaningful a popular 'Yes' or 'No' would be on what was likely to prove so complex an instrument. Such precautions, however, faithfully represent the delicacy with which military administrations tread in the re-approach to politics: it is as though they are subconsciously restrained from decisiveness to the extent of making the operation virtually impossible. Nevertheless the efforts made from the first by the N.L.C. in Ghana, like the Alley régime in Dahomey, to return by logical and carefully inhibited steps to civilian rule deserved credit in that such measures by the military are comparatively rare and indicated

L

perhaps the degree of popular political sophistication which had been frustrated during the earlier civilian periods.

The results of the ingenuity of the constitution makers are, however, only a prelude to the real thing – the provision of a framework and arena for the political gladiators who have yet to emerge or re-emerge into the limelight. In Ghana there was at the time of the appointment of the electoral commissioner little popular enthusiasm for abdication by the N.L.C., only perhaps some cynicism about its success in dealing with the economic crisis and restoring world confidence in the country. The functioning of the ministries under civilian commissioners seemed to be a success and had effectively created a vested interest among many senior civil servants in the continuance of disciplined order. The image of the Ghana régime in the first two years of its existence owed a great deal to the integration of the élite in the public services. In so far as potential politicians had begun to re-emerge and show their anxiety for a return to civilian government they were largely associated with the old opposition groups. The dangers in the intervening period were clearly that political parties would reform underground and that elections for the constituent assembly even if they were to be on a non-party basis would be contested by individuals who were less free of group obligations than they appeared to be. The possibility of such a crystallization of opinions during the middle period of office of a military régime must place a particular strain on the relationships within its controlling council and, more especially, within the security forces.

These were the problems which the Sierra Leone affair brightly illuminated precisely because the coup of March 1967 could be regarded as having been an unnecessary interference with the political processes – with, in fact, the first substantial example in tropical Africa of a change of government by constitutional electoral process. The defeat of Sir Albert Margai's Sierra Leone Peoples' Party (S.L.P.P.), in spite of the desperate attempts of the party to remain in power by fraud, and the succession to the premiership of Mr Siaka Stevens at the invitation of the Governor-General were quickly set at naught by the intervention of Brigadier David Lansana, Commander of the Army. He in turn was rapidly displaced by a rising of younger army officers who claimed, as Lansana had also done, that the situation was likely to produce tribal conflict, in particular between the Mende and Temne peoples. There is no doubt in this case that informed popular opinion, far from being relieved by the efficient intervention of the military, felt intensely politically thwarted by it. The subsequent history of the Juxon-Smith National Reformation Council (N.R.C.) which took over the administration illustrated clearly the problems of a return to civilian rule even in a situation where, as the Dove-Edwin Commission of Enquiry into the election decided, a valid alternative government already existed: there was, the Commission said, no need for a further general election and the great majority of those elected and of the electorate certainly agreed. After the Dove-Edwin report any prolongation of matters by the N.R.C. was bound to be seen as procrastination designed to facilitate the retention of power where it did not legally belong. There was, for instance, emphasis on the possibility of a national government which for obvious reasons could not be a coalition of the two major parties. The subsequent three months or so brought to a head the criticism of the military which had prevailed since the start.

What little the N.R.C. had done for the country's economic and financial recovery was obscured essentially by the nature of the coup and of the acquired characteristics of Brigadier Juxon-Smith's authority. He held office at the wish of the original coup leaders merely on grounds of seniority, but anyone who had known him as a cadet or young officer in Britain or Sierra Leone appreciated that he had not the qualities of a statesman or the professionalism of an Afrifa or Gowon. Unlike his opposite numbers elsewhere in English-speaking West Africa he antagonized his military colleagues, the senior civil servants, and the police. His arbitrary behaviour suggested his enjoyment of power, and his commitment to a return to civilian rule was regarded as insincere because of his continual references to the ways in which the politicians would be kept in check. His unwillingness to act towards the appointment of a Siaka Stevens government, after the Dove-Edwin report, led to the deduction that he would only accept a Margai-type government back.

The weakness of his and the N.R.C.'s position was exacerbated by marked failure to live up to the reputation of military régimes for cleaning up corruption. The gestures were made but ruined by members of the N.R.C. who themselves at least appeared to profit from office. They failed too to cope with large-scale diamond smuggling, itself a prominent source of corruption. Above all, the motives of the original coup leaders had not been primarily the safeguarding of the national interest. It was the personal incompetence of Brigadier Lansana and his identification with tribal, political interests which incensed them. Lansana was by far the most senior of all Sierra Leonean officers, having been commissioned for years before other Africans joined him in the regimental mess. He had had time to develop political connections during the colonial period and he inherited an army notable for its appalling barracks at Wilberforce and its practically non-existent welfare and medical services. Failure to cope with these deficiencies led both to his downfall and in due course to that of the N.R.C. It was not surprising, therefore, that in the event the men of the Sierra Leone Military Forces preferred to act for a return to civilian rule. In so doing they returned to authority two of the more competent officers, Colonel John Bangura, a Temne, and Lieutenant-Colonel Ambrose Genda, and imprisoned the rest. The process of returning to civilian rule at the end of April 1968 was in the event carried out with remarkable precision and efficiency.

The appointment of Mr Siaka Stevens as Prime Minister led

to the appointment of other ministers and the formal abolition
of the interim administration which itself had replaced the
Anti-Corruption Revolutionary Council formed by the counter-
coup leaders. The Chief Justice acted as the officer-administer-
ing the Constitution in lieu of the Governor-General. In the
end a national government with S.L.P.P. representation was
formed and the whole given the appropriate cloak of legality.[1]

The military situation which made the return to civilian
rule possible seems to have been created at an unusually low
level in the ranks of the Army. The key figure[2] seems to have
been a young Temne radio operator, Morlai Kamara, stationed
at Daru but with the opportunity to visit Wilberforce Barracks.
He and his associates were apparently motivated by discontent
with their pay – about £15 a month – and allowances in the
face of the rumoured self-enrichment of the N.R.C. régime.
Their objective was a total change of officers by initiating action at Daru, and this they achieved by persuading certain
N.C.O.s and Warrant officers to co-operate, and in so doing
they brought to political power Siaka Stevens, one of the few
longstanding politicians in Africa in the trades union tradition.
Thus the original Sierra Leone coup leaders, and the N.R.C.
which they formed, disregarded in a unique fashion the recipe
for a successful coup. They seized power for predominantly
selfish reasons and in so doing thwarted the popular political
will. In power they failed to live up to the image of the upright
patriotic soldier and thus provoked an other-rank rising of a
kind which has rarely been successful. In so doing they ex-
emplified in a negative fashion the characteristics of military
intervention in politics in modern Africa and the difficulties
involved in engineering a transfer back to civilian rule even
though, in their case, the route was already demarcated. By
interfering with political evolution, however briefly and ac-

---

[1] For a detailed account see *West Africa*, No. 2657 of 4 May 1968,
pp. 506–7.
[2] *West Africa*, op. cit.

cidentally, they showed clearly that while the Army is the convenient agent for the suspension of activities in a deteriorating situation, it is inherently unsuited for the task of political reorientation, and when it fails even for a time to 'clean-up' the administration it may become a force tending to encourage instability rather than the reverse.

In retrospect the relative political quiescence of African armies in the first three years of the 1960s deceived observers into false contrasts with other developing areas. Political intervention during this period was scarcely a practicable activity: expatriate influence in the forces remained and key posts were often in foreign hands. The rate of Africanization and adaptation of the armed forces was slower than in other public services. This factor in itself was a source of some unrest, as in East Africa. Coups took place as armies gained confidence and disillusionment with politicians became endemic. The armed forces had to acquire status as national institutions and dispel their imperial image before they could come to be regarded as patriotic champions of order and normality. Unlike their counterparts in Latin America they had not been forged in a liberation struggle: they were small and generally directly inherited from the colonial era. Their rise and the consolidation of their position nationally – sometimes assisted, as in the cases of Ghana and Nigeria, by a sound record of service with the U.N. in the Congo – coincided with the decline of the independence governments.

The problems of these governments derived partly from the difficulty of maintaining an appearance of national and party unity after the need to 'fight' the colonial power had gone. Divisions in the parties and militant opposition led to repression and aroused the naïve political emotions of those military men who were imbued with a respect for Western democratic traditions and practices. Once one or two coups had been successful, confidence mounted, partly due to the realization that outside intervention was unlikely, except in one or two

Francophone countries. Chronic economic problems and corruption provided the background, which helped to suggest to army leaders that they not only had the power to intervene but also administrative skills and other qualities which were, as it were, in short supply. They often intervened as a 'corrective' measure, but almost invariably without policies. To a limited degree they have justified their administrative claims, but the evolution of policy and the discovery of a new basis for legitimacy have proved elusive.

Short Bibliography

AFRIFA, COLONEL A. A., *The Ghana Coup*, London, 1966.

ALEXANDER, MAJOR GENERAL H. T., C.B., C.B.E., D.S.O., *African Tightrope*, London, 1965.

BELL, M. J. V., *Army and Nation in Sub Saharan Africa*, Adelphi Paper No. 21, Institute for Strategic Studies, 1965.

FINER, S. E., *The Man on Horseback*, London, 1962; New York, 1963.

GUTTERIDGE, WILLIAM F., *Armed Forces in New States*, London and New York, 1962.

GUTTERIDGE, WILLIAM F., 'Education of Military Leadership in Emergent States' in ed. COLEMAN, JAMES S. *Education and Political Development*, Princeton, 1965.

GUTTERIDGE, WILLIAM F., *Military Institutions and Power in the New States*, London, 1965.

GUTTERIDGE, WILLIAM F., *The Political Role of African Armed Forces: The Impact of Foreign Military Assistance*, in African Affairs Vol. 66, No. 263, April 1967.

HAYWOOD, COLONEL A., C.M.G., C.B.E., D.S.O. and CLARKE, BRIGADIER F. A. S., D.S.O., *The History of the Royal West African Frontier Force*, Aldershot, 1964.

JANOWITZ, MORRIS, *The Military in the Political Development of New States*, Chicago, 1964.

JOHNSON, JOHN J. (ED)., *The Role of the Military in Underdeveloped Countries*, Princeton, 1962.

MOYSE-BARTLETT, LIEUTENANT-COLONEL H., *The King's African Rifles*, Aldershot, 1956.

SUTTON, JOHN L. and KEMP, GEOFFREY, *Arms to Developing*

Countries 1945–65, Adelphi Paper No. 28, Institute for Strategic Studies, London, 1966.

—— *West Africa.*

WOOD, DAVID and GUTTERIDGE, WILLIAM F., *The Armed Forces of African States*, Adelphi Paper No. 27, Institute for Strategic Studies, London, 1966.

Index